LARGER THAN LIFE
The Biography of Robert Morley

by Margaret Morley

 Robson Books

The publishers are grateful to the Morley family for providing a number of the photos in this book, and to the British Film Institute for their help — also to the following for permission to reprint particular photos: British Lion Film Corporation (*You Will Remember*), 20th Century Production (*The Young Mr Pitt*), Associated British Picture Corporation (*I Live in Grosvenor Square* and *The Young Ones*), Bert Wilson (*The First Gentleman*), Angus McBean (*A Likely Tale*), Cinemabilia, NYC (*Beat The Devil*), MGM (*The Journey* and *Marie Antoinette*), Columbia (*Cromwell*), Harbour Productions (*Theatre of Blood*), Dave Willis (with Diana Rigg), Daily Express (Gladys Cooper's eightieth birthday), Ben Martin (summer lunch at Fairmans), GTO Films (*Too Many Chefs*).

FIRST PUBLISHED IN GREAT BRITAIN IN 1979 BY ROBSON BOOKS LTD., 28 POLAND STREET, LONDON W1V 3DB. COPYRIGHT © 1979 MARGARET MORLEY.

Morley, Margaret
  Larger than life.
  1. Morley, Robert   2. Actors – Great Britain –
  Biography
  I. Title
  792'.028'0924   PN2598.M67

    ISBN 0 86051 064 6

Printed and bound in Great Britain by
R. J. Acford Ltd., Industrial Estate, Chichester, Sussex

LARGER THAN LIFE

For Robert, With Love

When I began this book, in celebration of Robert's seventieth birthday and as a present (what do you give the man who has everything?) I told him I didn't want to hear a word from him. After all, I had read his books, known him for fourteen years and heard his version. I wanted to know the facts, unembroidered, and hear other people's views. But are facts ever unembroidered? Most of Robert's friends told me of the fun he inspired around him — fun I had often experienced — and they were also helpful as to versions of well-told tales although agreement among them was seldom reached. Time and point of view impede memories. Great thanks are due to all of them and to Joan, my mother-in-law, who kept numbers of Robert's letters through the years and lent them to me. Also, of course, to Sheridan, my husband, who is a mine of historical theatrical information — and saved endless searching for just the right source. A special thanks to the following people who either wrote their memories or gave me interviews:

Michael Blakemore, Margaret (Morley) Bucknall, Peter Bull, Peter Cadbury, Rosalind Chatto, Meriel Forbes, Angela Fox, Morton Gottlieb, Ian McCulloch, Richard O'Donoghue, Julian Orchard, Ambrosine Phillpotts, Llewellyn Rees, Nevil E. Schooling, Sewell Stokes, Tom Sowerby, Horace West, Norman Wright, Frank Fisher, Mark Baker and Yvonne Spawforth of Wellington College, The staff of the British Film Institute and Leicester Square Libraries.

PREFACE

'GOOD MORNING, my dear. Would you like toast or a bath?'
It was Boxing Day morning, 1964 when I met Robert
Morley for the first time, and those were his first words. It
should perhaps be explained that it was, in context, not such
a strange greeting because I had spent the night crossing the
Atlantic on an aeroplane. It was my first such flight and I
probably looked the worse for it. I had met his elder son,
Sheridan, the previous year in Hawaii where we were both
doing graduate work at the university, and now I had come
to 'meet the family'. I arrived with feelings of some
trepidation as I couldn't imagine what to expect. My image
of Robert had been formed mainly from what I had seen of
him on television talk shows, eccentric, witty, complaining
about schools and ball games; and also from the role of a
bumbling crook he had played in *Beat the Devil*.
I had prepared myself for Hollywood-style grandeur (after
all, Sheridan's mother was Gladys Cooper's daughter), for a
very British country house with scrambled eggs and kippers
in silver dishes on the sideboard (Robert's image was very
much the English gentleman), or for a slightly Bohemian
catch-as-catch-can residence (actors are a notoriously
peculiar lot). But I found none of these. Fairmans, the family
home since before Sheridan was born, was (and is) a cosy,
warm, medium-sized house, painted white with blue
shutters, and I found Robert and his wife Joan in the kitchen
preparing toast and coffee for breakfast. I sighed, deeply
relieved — it was very like home.

7

Sheridan and I married the following summer and I came to live in England. Sunday lunches and often long weekends were spent at Fairmans. As a Morley I learned the family habit of eating very quickly indeed and keeping the conversation going at the same time. Robert introduced me to film sets, theatre dressing-rooms, racing and roulette, and as the children arrived he became a willing and amusing baby-sitter — for short stretches. Occasionally he was to be seen pushing the pram the three miles to the village with one hand while guiding a toddler with the other. Usually, though, he couldn't face the journey back and he and his charges had to be fetched in the car from the riverside pub where they had sought refuge.

Robert has proved never at a loss to provide amusement for any one, whether family, friend or acquaintance. The only trouble with him is that it is impossible to buy presents for him. Like a child, he can never hide his disappointment if the Christmas offering is found boring or the birthday tie not quite the right shade.

MARGARET MORLEY, 1979

8

CHAPTER ONE

SOME PEOPLE DO NOT MAKE very good children. They should spring upon the world fully grown, preferably with a gin and tonic in hand, a conversation in full swing, and a camera equipped with sound on the premises to record the event. Childhood is for them a waiting game they never asked to play and one whose rules they neither accept nor indeed ever quite understand. Most people come to terms with this and give in — others won't or can't, so the period from birth to majority becomes one of agony. To none of their peers can they relate. Children's conversation is meaningless and school merely entrenches the horror.

But there can be no exceptions to the rule of nature. Everyone must be born and mature in the accepted fashion, so Robert Adolph Wilton Morley was born on Tuesday, May 26th in 1908. Years later, from the shape of his head, a doctor suggested that Robert must have had a difficult birth; his mother replied when asked about it that she had indeed noticed. Robert was born into a family that consisted of a mother, a father, a sister and assorted servants. Father had probably recently decided to try his hand at becoming a gentleman farmer, because the winter before the birth they had moved from Folkestone with the baby, Margaret, to a farmhouse in the village of Semley in Wiltshire. However, before the year was out the expanded family moved back to Folkestone to the bow-windowed, turreted houses of the fashionable Augusta Gardens. Father had given up the idea

9

of being a farmer, one of the many ideas he had tried out and rejected — and there were still many more to come.

Major Robert Wilton Morley had been born in 1866. He had attended Wellington College and become an officer in the Fourth Royal Irish Dragoon Guards. Although he had retired around the turn of the century he went back for the Boer War. Major Morley had a brother, Basil, and two sisters, Evelyn and Constance. (A third sister, Beatrice, lived only four and a half months.) The Morley family lived a very comfortable life in Courtfield Gardens, Kensington, next door to the Fass family, who were equally comfortable. Both families seem to have made money trekking in South Africa, and the Morleys headed the London Parcel Service.

The Fass family was decidedly larger. Father was Adolph, who had been born in Germany but went to Natal, South Africa, to make his fortune when he was seventeen. It was there, in 1863, that he married Sophie Gade. The family began to arrive in 1864. First Bertha, then Elizabeth, Adolph and Edith. In 1872 came Gertrude Emily whom the family called Daisy, or more often 'poor Daisy'. She viewed herself as rather the 'put-upon' member of the family. Then there was Sophie — and Frank, Ernest, Reggie and Gracie. The Fasses also had a large country house in Chalfont St Peter. The Morleys and Fasses were constantly in and out of each other's houses and up and down to the Grange in Chalfont, and the handsome young officer fell in love with Edith. A match was discouraged because Major Morley, though well-bred, well-educated and very well placed, had a major flaw: money fell through his open fingers. It disappeared on the roulette table, on the baize bridge tables, and it galloped away on the horses. Sadly, he actually believed in 'hot tips'. He was not a responsible person. Edith married Sir George Armstrong, altogether a more suitable mate. But Daisy, who had become her parents' indispensable housekeeper, was attracted to the charming and amusing gentleman, and after Edith had gone, he noticed her. On January 9th, 1906, amid prophesies of doom, Gertrude Emily Fass became Mrs Morley at All Saints' Church, Ennismore Gardens. The

10

family no longer referred to her as 'poor Daisy'. Now they would speak of 'poor, poor Daisy'.

Major Morley was 40 and his bride was 34. They were of totally dissimilar character. He was outgoing and gregarious, always ready to try something new. He was certainly no respecter of money or tradition. For a time he had been on the staff of the Viceroy of India and wished ever afterwards to continue to live a champagne life — although he had only a beer income. Daisy was, like many ladies of her day, solitary, shy, and subject to attacks of the vapours. One of her sisters noted that she was the kind of woman who would lie all day on the sofa, eating chocolates and reading a huge romantic novel. At the end of the day she would be thoroughly depressed because she was not the heroine of the novel. Yet, as is so often fatally the case, opposites attracted and they were very much in love.

Just over a year later Margaret was born, and the following year, Robert. They were to become known as little Cissie and little Bobbie. After his difficult birth, Robert became a delicate child subject to chest ailments and biliousness. The local doctor attributed the bilious attacks to vast over-eating. His parents were horrified. The child was delicate and needed to keep his strength up. Whatever the cause of his delicate condition, he was immensely over-coddled by worrying parents. In those days, before antibiotics, childish complaints often blew up dangerously, and the middle-aged parents were taking no chances. Father was restless but for a few years movement was confined within Folkestone — Augusta Gardens, Clifton Crescent, Earls Avenue, with the occasional visits to Chalfont to the family home.

The Fass family made great efforts to keep poor Daisy's money out of the Major's hands; he'd already gone through his own. Sometimes these efforts were successful but as often as not they weren't. He was an accomplished actor, and his pitiful condition usually brought capitulations. There was always a drama in the house, and the drama was usually about money. There was also the nanny, Nurse Gilbert, a great believer in milk puddings, whose favourite song was *Once in Royal David's City*. She would sing two verses of it while she bathed the children and one while she dried them.

Although there was no shortage of adoring and very generous aunts and uncles, the constant upheaval of the family left the children with few friends so they turned to each other and became very close, although Cissie felt strongly that she was usually made to give in to Bobbie because he was younger, and besides he was delicate. Mother fussed a lot about health and the children spent a good deal of time with their noses pressed against the window panes, longing to get out. Still, Folkestone was a good place to be in those days before the Great War. It had been slow in developing as a fashionable spot, but when in the 1890s it did, it soon overtook its rival seaside spas. Royalty often came to visit and Society was very much in evidence. It always grieved Daisy that, owing, she felt, to her husband's eccentricities, the family never quite belonged. Yet there were teas and the social calls. For the children it was a splendid place to be. There was the sea and the lift from the high-up Leas right down to the beach, and there were wonderful bands — sometimes three or four playing in a single day. All the grand people could be seen promenading, on foot or in their Bath chairs. Folkestone was refined, genteel, tidy and for a child, exciting. The West End, where they lived in various houses, was full of PLUs ('people like us' — a phrase used by the gentry of the period to distinguish the 'U' from the 'non-U'), and very aware of its position. It was here that little Bobbie formed not so much his idea of himself but, perhaps unconsciously, his idea of the people he wanted to impress when he was finally allowed outside the green baize door of the nursery. These were the people he wanted to take notice of him and approve. Praise was not readily forthcoming at home. Mother took her duties as an Edwardian mother very seriously. She would not spoil her children emotionally. Praise was something that had to be earned, and the children seldom achieved enough to warrant it. The goals were constantly being extended out of

12

reach. That was how empires were built. Neither parent was overly religious — though church-going was still a social necessity for the PLU. However, Major Morley had a bible. It was Rudyard Kipling's poem, *If*. This was frequently recited and became deeply imbedded in the children's minds. In moments of stress — and on plenty of other occasions as well — Robert still recites it.

Resources must have been low in 1912 because most of that year was spent back at Chalfont. Yet no matter how poor 'poor Daisy' felt she was, most winters she managed her holidays in the South of France. This was of course for her health, which worried her nearly as much as the children's did. It was also about this time that little Bobbie was taken to Switzerland to have his tonsils out. He was given a box of conjuring tricks for being good about the operation. Perhaps it would cure his delicate condition, and the doctors in Switzerland were deemed to be best at this kind of thing and the climate was so good for recuperation. Besides, on the continent Father was closer to the gambling casinos. The tonsils grew back. Still, Bobbie had his birthday there and was presented with a splendid cake with white sugar doves all around the edge. Margaret's eyes lit up when she saw it. Oh, could she have one of those lovely doves? No, because she had asked, and that wasn't polite. It wasn't easy being a child when refinement and self-control were everything.

It was back to Folkestone, and then Father had a brilliant idea. The scheme had something to do with money — making it, that is. Major Morley wasn't overly interested in conserving what they had. The entire family packed up and moved to St Peter's Port in Guernsey. Upon arrival Father decided he didn't like it, and after a few days he was on the boat back to England. The rest of them stayed three months; long enough for Bobbie to be sent to a dame school there. Schools never lasted very long: either the pupils or the teachers or the meals were never quite right for these precious children. Little Bobbie soon cottoned on to his parents' attitude and managed to hate every school to which he was sent. And he usually got himself removed in a term or two. After all, he wasn't used to other children. He and Margaret had always been on their own. How horrifying it must have been to be confronted with the rough and tumble of a bunch of boys after the refined, though dramatic environment of home life. When he was first sent away to prep school, as all little boys of his class and generation had to be, his parents returned home and cried inconsolably. Margaret, finding it bad enough to be without her little brother and constant companion, decided that her dismal parents' pining for their absent son was the last straw and begged to be allowed to go away too.

Guernsey abandoned, they returned to England but Folkestone was no place to spend the war. Barbed wire covered the beaches, zeppelins dropped bombs and the town was full of troops heading for the continent. The Morleys rented a house in the grounds of Wellington College in Crowthorne, Berkshire. Daisy and the Major had a mutual passion for Tiptree jams and, fearing a shortage, had loaded a goodly supply into the loft. The children spent the war worrying that they would be arrested for hoarding. A strange noise in the night, and they would whisper to each other, 'They've found the jam', and hide under the bedclothes.

The Major wrote a moving short story about a vicar who found himself very busy one afternoon dealing with the rather picayune problems of his parishioners. He handled each of them with tact and gentleness, all the while keeping in his pocket the telegram informing him that his only son had been killed in France. The story was never published but remains in manuscript, copied out in a strong, attractive style. Had he ever submitted it for publication? He wasn't averse to selling things, but it was usually the silver. There was the time he put an advertisement in *The Times*: 'Is there an afterlife? Send a guinea to Major Morley c/o Box No. . . .' There was not a great number of replies and sadly his answer is no longer extant.

The war changed a lot of things and society especially was disrupted. By the end of the hostilities the Morleys had sold all their furniture and the various moves now took them to furnished premises, hotels and clubs. But still these homes were in fashionable areas. They lived in London for a time. It was here that Robert returned from one of his numerous prep schools very seriously ill with influenza. So high was he in his feverous state that he didn't realize how ill he was until he saw the distraught look on the faces of his parents as they nursed him. It frightened him into recovering.

The Major decided to be a restauranteur, and opened Wilton's Coffee House off the Kensington High Street. Despite — or maybe because of — the fact that he had Margaret and Robert sitting at the pavement tables, trying to look jolly, it was not a success. Summer holidays found them back at the seaside, at Bognor or on the Isle of Wight at Totland Bay. But Daisy was happier in Folkestone and she returned there whenever possible.

Wallace Harold Elliott was the vicar of Holy Trinity Church, a carpeted and golden edifice built in 1868 for the West End of Folkestone. Little Bobbie found his preaching extremely dramatic and very exhilarating and his first stage performance was under Canon Elliott's direction in a Christmas play written by the versatile vicar in 1920. Margaret had a smaller part and was very jealous. It was not on this occasion, however, that Bobbie decided on his future, though the decision was made in Folkestone in the following year.

Robert's school of that year was located in Folkestone, and one day the boys were given a half-day holiday. Robert has always maintained that the holiday was declared in celebration of the delight the masters had at finally getting him through the public school examinations. While the other boys hurried off to the cricket pavilion, Robert took himself to the Pleasure Gardens Theatre. The theatre had started life as an exhibition hall with a glass roof and spacious galleries along the lines of the Crystal Palace. Somehow the townspeople and visitors were not attracted to it. In 1888 it was converted into a theatre seating one thousand people. Few of those seats were occupied at the matinee where Robert saw George Bernard Shaw's *The*

Doctor's Dilemma. Esme Percy was playing Dubedat. Percy was a short plump man with a broken nose. He also had an amazing vocal range and he delighted in the elaborate speeches Shaw wrote. And at that sparse matinee performance he proclaimed Dubedat's creed to perfection. 'I know that in an accidental sort of way, struggling through the unreal part of life, I haven't always been able to live up to my ideal. But in my own real world I have never done anything wrong, never denied my faith, never been untrue to myself. I've been threatened and blackmailed and insulted and starved, but I've played the game. I've fought the good fight. And now it's all over, there's an indescribable peace. I believe in Michaelangelo, Velasquez and Rembrandt; in the might of design, the mystery of colour, the redemption of all things by Beauty everlasting and the message of Art that has made these hands blessed.' That was it. Robert felt himself transformed that afternoon. He knew what he wanted to do with his life.

However, although his future was firmly determined in his own mind, there still loomed ahead Wellington College. Bobbie was sure that English Public School would be no better than English Prep School and probably a lot worse. He was installed in Wellesley House in the summer term of 1922. Living in a house had advantages over living in college. A house was looked after by a master and his wife. Thirty-six boys resided there, giving it more of a family atmosphere than college which numbered boys in hundreds and was really a dormitory existence. Besides, the meals were much better in the houses than in the college dining-room. How did you get into a house? Well, it cost more money. As in all public shools of the day, discipline was strict. As one of Robert's contemporaries at Wellington remembered, 'All the masters were in the mould of muscular Christianity invented by Dr Arnold of Rugby.' And Wellington with its military traditions was as tough as most and more so than some. Although the grounds were beautiful — rolling grassland, a lake, and magnificent rhododendrons — the buildings were the essence of Victoriana — solid imposing

16

and claustrophobic. Dark wood panels absorbed any sunlight that managed to slip through the inadequate windows. To Robert it was a prison. However, although he now denies it, he made the best of his time there. Military corps was of course compulsory (unless you could convince them you were a bona fide Quaker — and with a Major for a father, Bobbie didn't stand a chance). All that marching was depressing. Robert wasn't exactly flat-footed yet he gave the impression of being so. Still, on parade he managed to pull faces and reduce his classmates to helpless laughter and although he now declares the invention of the ball to be the most dreadful disaster to befall the human race, he is remembered as a rather good rugger player by those who were with him in the scrum.

He was interested in poetry and literature, and was always sending compositions to the college magazine, *The Wellingtonian*, for publication. But the magazine at that time was almost entirely a record of events — there were very few literary articles. It was about the dullest school magazine in the country. There is no record of Robert being published in it, apart from the possibility that a letter (all signatures were pen-names) which suggested the formation of a drama society and signed 'Yours with customary apologies — Whynot', was his.

Dr Lemmy was the master of Wellesley house, and would invite four boys at a time to dinner with his family. The boys had the usual school-boy names for the Doctor's daughters. The object of these dinners was to foster the social graces. The other boys found it a great relief to be invited on the same evening as Bobbie Morley. He managed to dominate the conversation, allowing them to get on with eating, merely nodding now and then and smiling, and saying nothing that would betray their boyish shyness. Bobbie was never dull. One evening he regaled the company with the story of his summer holiday in Dinard in France, where he was introduced to the art of fishing, and managed to get a fish-hook caught in his hand. Gesturing, he had tried to explain to onlookers that he was worried about being poisoned by the metal. Unfortunately, owing to his hysteria and the inadequacies of his schoolboy French, the crowd understood him to be exclaiming about his 'poisson', and kept looking for a magnificent catch.

The matron who looked after him at Wellesley House was a Miss Beverly. She was a no-nonsense Scots lady who would verbally attack visiting parents with 'We've no time for fussy mothers here.' Poor Daisy found this very daunting. Miss Beverly also presided at the bridge table, to which various boys would be invited at tea-time. She was a very good bridge player and would sit the boys down in fours and prowl behind them instructing them on the art of bridge as she studied their cards. Most of the boys attended only because they dared not do otherwise — and besides the tea was extravagant — sandwiches, sausages and cakes enough to make the adolescent heart succumb even to bridge.

Robert is remembered by his school mates as boisterous, pleasant and amusing. There was no sign of the sulking, miserable chap he will inevitably describe if asked about his time at Wellington. There was no poor soul cowering in the corners in fear of the masters. Perhaps he was already mastering his chosen profession. Wellesley House was some distance from the main part of the college. Classmates remember him standing on the steps in the morning, books under his arm, and his size lending weight to his authority as he called 'Wait on — I shall accompany you to class.' The recipient of the command always waited. It made for an interesting walk.

At the end of each term all the boys in the form were lined up and asked by the master what they planned to do with their lives. The greatest suspense was usually whether the boy would say Army or Navy and what rank he intended to achieve. Very occasionally a boy would say he was going into business and explain how he intended to make a fortune. Then it came to Robert's turn. Very bravely he told the truth: 'I am going on the stage.' There were puzzled looks all round. 'Ah, well, we must all suffer our eccentrics,' the master said as he dismissed the assembly.

Robert did not stay the course at Wellington. It was not surprising. He had never stayed the course at any school. He remembers leaving because he was very ill — it was in December of 1924. His classmates remember his leaving as due to a family financial crisis. 'Poor Papa,' he told one of them, 'it's not his fault.'

Whatever the reason, school was at last mercifully over. But Bobbie, being only sixteen, couldn't actually be set loose on the world. In 1924 in his class it just wasn't done. He continued in his ambition to be an actor. It was an ambition that was rather frowned upon by Mother, who had always hoped her son would be 'something in the Empire'. Father wasn't quite so upset by the idea of his son going on the stage, but felt that he should be shown some alternatives. Travel was said to broaden the mind, so he set out to broaden Bobbie's. Culling a bit of money from the estate in the name of education the two of them would set out for the continent. Full of good intentions they would begin with Paris or Florence and inevitably end up in Deauville or Monte Carlo. The money would disappear in a day or two on the roulette tables, and they would be quickly home again making all kinds of plans and schemes to secure some more money to continue Bobbie's education. Yet, miraculously, twice during this time Bobbie was actually settled abroad. As he has described it: 'Father once settled me in Alassio on the Italian Riveria where there wasn't the smell of a casino and where I was supposed to learn Italian in the house of an irritable English Colonel who spoke not a word of Italian himself. Here I spent endless afternoons at the English tennis club pretending I was going to play later. One day the Colonel said to me, "Morley, you're a fool; it's a perfect waste of time trying to teach you anything and I shall write to your father and tell him so." But I was the one who wrote to my father a report of this conversation, which resulted in my being withdrawn instantly . . . What made the Colonel's frankness so commendable, if reckless, was that I was his only pupil and we both subsequently travelled home together.' The unfortunate Colonel did not find Robert's sophisticated pea-shooter very endearing, and indeed had once been nearly blinded by it.

After the Italian fiasco the family decided to try Germany, and Bobbie was sent to stay with a German banking family in Hanover. He was supposed to go each day to the university to take lessons in the language, but found other distractions much more interesting than the study of German. There were weekly outings to look at Hindenburg, who wasn't yet president of the Reich but 'a splendid old gentleman he looked' and was very popular. There was also motor racing, to which his host was addicted — preferably when there was lots of blood. There seemed to be a good deal of bloodiness about in Hanover at the time. There was the trial of the Mass-Murderer-of-Hanover who was reputed to have sold his many victims to the local butcher after disposing of the identifiably human bits into a fast moving ravine. Robert has remained fascinated by the macabre — as long as it is at a safe distance. Bobbie was less taken with the custom of duelling which was still regarded as great sport among the students of Hanover.In fact they would rub salt into their wound to make the scars more prominent. This game, played by his acquaintances, was too close for comfort. During this time Bobbie spoke only German. He returned home, retained not a word of the foreign tongue, and his family gave up trying to educate him. Still, if they were so horrified at the idea of his going on the stage, he was willing to think up an alternative. He was a dutiful child. While he was on one of his journeys abroad he had met a man called Leslie Clark who was a director of Amalgamated Press, and had thought that journalism might be a very attractive profession. No sooner did Bobbie mention that to his father than he was whisked off to an appointment with Lord Astor, then the owner of *The Times*. If nothing else, Bobbie's family always had a 'friend at Court'. They moved in the right circles and there was always a friend of a friend . . . Lord Astor couldn't have been more charming, more helpful, more interested in the young man. Bobbie left the interview thinking he would be appointed at least foreign correspondent. A few weeks later a letter arrived saying how pleased they would be to recommend him as a temporary cub on a provincial paper.

By this time Daisy and the Major were more or less separated. Daisy was living in Kent with Margaret who, Robert felt, had become inordinately fond of cows and chickens, but she was understandably happy to have a permanent residence. The Major was living in the Strand Palace Hotel. Bobbie had no trouble deciding where to live. He hated the country and moved into the Strand Palace with father, and at last auditioned for a place at the Royal Academy of Dramatic Art.

CHAPTER TWO

THE ROYAL ACADEMY OF DRAMATIC ART had been the brainchild of Sir Herbert Beerbohm Tree, an immensely controversial actor-manager. He was criticized for his odd personality, his throaty delivery and his bizarre gestures. Yet his productions were major theatrical events noted for their splendour and realism. Rabbits burrowed through the scenery in his production of *A Midsummer Night's Dream,* and he actually rode a horse on stage in *Richard II* through a reconstruction of London. He was managing the Haymarket Theatre at the age of 34 and ten years later he crossed the road and built his own theatre, Her Majesty's, mostly with the profits from his enormous success, *Trilby,* in which he played Svengali. He was a tall, lanky, blue-eyed man, notoriously vague about details like money and where the other actors should stand on stage, but he had great tenacity of purpose and faith in his own ideas, and one idea he was devoted to was that London needed a school for actors founded along the lines of the Paris Conservatoire. In 1904 he founded just such a school at his own theatre (renamed His Majesty's on the accession of Edward VII). Applications flooded in, mostly from stage-struck young ladies, and what with the rabbits and birds and horses — not to mention thunder and lightning machines and ship-wrecked boats for *The Tempest* — it all got out of hand. Most of the 'students' had come to be near the great Beerbohm Tree and the results were not encouraging. A fellow manager once told Tree that he had one of his students in his company. 'You are lucky,' Tree replied, 'I've got two.'

Tree still believed in his idea; he just had to get the school out of his theatre. He found premises in Gower Street where he more or less abandoned it — except for the stipulation that under 'Academy of Dramatic Art' (the 'Royal' was not granted until 1920) should appear the words 'founded by H. B. Tree in 1904'.

By the time Robert arrived for his entrance test on September 29th, 1926, things were more orderly. The building next door had been acquired. A theatre had been built on the premises and a new building was in the planning stages. All this had been accomplished under the administration of Kenneth Barnes who had been in charge since 1909 — except for the war years. There was indeed an entrance test; Robert recited from *Don Juan* by Flecker — a strange choice, perhaps. One of the examining committee at the audition laughed at this serious piece and was so overcome with guilt that Robert was admitted to begin classes on October 1st. There was an advantage to being male since applicants were predominantly female: that year 52 girls were accepted and 16 men. A motley group they were, too. There was a businessman who had a penchant for tap dancing, a widow who kept her husband's ashes on the mantelpiece, and a girl who reminded everyone of a little pig but who could perform music-hall sketches and songs to perfection. One of the first activities after entrance was the competition for a scholarship. The judges that year were Athole Stewart, Eva Moore (who was on the council) and Mary Barton (an actress who had won the RADA gold medal for acting in the public show of 1906). There was a very refined and meticulous system for judging — the top mark which could be given was 100 and it was divided thus: 25 for acting Shakespeare, 25 for acting modern, 15 for gesture, 15 for diction, 8 for voice production, 6 for dancing and 6 for fencing. Robert didn't gain a scholarship but he got above average marks. As his dancing and fencing weren't up to much he must have done very well in the other categories.

23

The work at the academy was not exactly onerous — especially not compared to the discipline of Wellington College. There was the opportunity to work if you wanted to, but there was plenty of time for the fun Robert delighted in. Although by Christmas he had managed to play the Magistrate in *The Silver Box,* Leonardo in *Much Ado About Nothing,* an elderly gentleman in *30 Minutes in the Street* and Colonel Jardin in *Mrs Gorringe's Necklace,* he had also perfected his ad-lib Shakespeare, to amuse his classmates, and found time for fun and games. Parents and friends were invited to the academy's theatre to see their offspring in performances. It was purely by invitation, but Robert and a friend called Charles Campbell thought a good opportunity was being lost and set up a box office to collect money from the hapless guests as they arrived. It didn't last very long as they were soon noticed by the staff.

Even in this first term the type of role he was going to be playing for the next ten years was well established — he was never going to be the juvenile lead — the romantic hero. That Christmas he found himself on the professional stage at last. Arthur Bourchier was presenting and starring in *Treasure Island* at the Strand Theatre. Bourchier had long been connected in a round about way with RADA. His first wife was Violet Vanbrugh, a distinguished actress who had played with Tree and who was also Kenneth Barnes's sister. Bourchier had given Barnes his first real job in the theatre when he asked him to translate and adapt a French play for his theatre, and he often found students from RADA to fill up the stage. Now he gave Robert his first job, as an elderly, lineless pirate. It was only one pound a week but it was the professional theatre and he approached it whole-heartedly — in fact there is a perhaps apochryphal family story that as Robert walked down Jermyn Street after securing the job he was approached by a lady of the streets who inquired professionally: 'Doing anything, love?' To which Robert, at least two feet off the ground replied, 'Yes, I'm a pirate at the Strand Theatre.'

Bourchier was not the easiest of leading men. Extras were

kept firmly in their place, and his second wife Kyrle Bellow helped him in this task. She was sitting in the front at a dress rehearsal. 'Arthur,' she called from the stalls, 'move that fat boy away from the gun. He spoils the picture.' So Robert was moved. Fat boy indeed! He was a ferocious pirate. Undeterred, he invented some business for himself. He lay dying on the stage while Bourchier as Long John Silver stood centre stage reading a letter. Ever so slowly Robert let a dagger fall from his lifeless hand. He managed this bit of upstaging six times before Bourchier noticed and had it stopped. He was at the best of times an irritable leading man. His dresser preceded him on stage calling 'Clear, please, for Mr Bourchier.' And as Long John Silver he was even more irritable since he never learned to manage with one leg tucked up. Once, in a rage at failing to open a door on the ship, he kicked a flat down. Robert vowed to be nicer to the cast when he was a star.

Back at the Royal Academy in February he returned to student life. Some of the people he respected most in the profession sat on the Council: Irene Vanbrugh (Kenneth Barnes's other sister who was married to Dion Bouccicault), George Bernard Shaw (whose writing after all had shown Robert the light) and Sir Gerald du Maurier, an actor of immense charm who had almost invented realistic personality acting. But these were not the people involved in the everyday life of the academy. At Gower Street daily there was Norman Page, who had been stage manager for Fay Compton in Barrie's plays and as an actor had specialized as a pantomime cat; and there was Elsie Chester, who tried hard to mould pupils into a pre-determined frame. Robert had decided early on that if anyone was going to mould him it was himself. No one other than himself seemed to be aware of his potential, but he maintains that he learned a lot at the academy: 'I didn't learn acting, but I learned patience, particularly from the lady who taught voice production, and I learned humility from Helen Haye who couldn't bear to watch us and would read the newspaper whenever we started to show off. "Not a winner in this lot," she would observe. "Perhaps I can spot one at Sandown Park." I learned, too, about makeup, and to this day place a spot of carmine in the extreme corner of each eyelid as recommended by Rosina Fillipi, and from my fellow students I learned that whether a man can act or not is really a matter of personal opinion (his own) and that in my personal opinion I was a better actor than a good many.'

It was Helen Haye, distracted from her racing for a time, who rehearsed him as Lord Elton in *The Last of Mrs Cheyney*. The character's name was changed to Lord Pifco as it turned out there was real Lord Elton who objected. Robert enjoyed playing in Lonsdale — that playwright was witty and articulate and created Robert's kind of role. By all accounts he was very good at it, too. But Robert's speciality at RADA was Shylock. He often performed the role using, when amusing his fellow students, his own version of Shakespearian dialogue which was indistinguishable from the original unless you listened carefully and realized he was talking double Dutch. It was the one part his mother could be persuaded to watch. Her reaction? 'Your fingernails were rather dirty.' On July 6th, 1927, he gave a performance of Shylock — the Tubal scene — before the students. At the end the audience cheered and cheered and went on clapping until Barnes got up and said, 'You might as well stop, he won't do it again.' Robert rather felt they were sending up his performance, but they were applauding not his Shylock but himself. They were applauding the sense of fun he brought everywhere with him.

Following his tradition of never quite completing any training scheme, Robert left the academy on July 21st, 1927, before the public show but not before he had been sent for by the administrator. Kenneth Barnes had strong ideas about the qualities that made a successful actor. 'Absolute concentration is imperative in acting. Every facet of the personality and of the physique must be trained to respond to the will of the actor. The spirit of self-discipline in thought word and deed alone enables students to discern with truth the emotional and moral values within themselves. The

26

outward expression of these human values constitutes the art of acting.' Now, there were some parts of his body which Robert barely communicated with, let alone controlled (Robert and a piece of sellotape, for instance, are inseparable), and he was not about to engage in soul-searching, at least not in public. Robert had been raised to have good manners, and had considered his mother's introspection as nothing short of gloominess. He would always be the antithesis of gloom. Why depress others? It wasn't really fair. He could look at himself and know he would never be Gerald du Maurier, he could analyse his techniques and know he would never be Forbes Robertson, and he was realistic enough about his ideas to know he would never be George Bernard Shaw. But never mind. It was useless to waste time trying to be someone else. He would be himself. He had his own talents to utilize.

'Do you have private means?' Kenneth Barnes enquired before Robert left the Academy. Robert assured him he was independently wealthy. Why worry the man — he had done his best. 'That relieves my mind a good deal,' Barnes replied, and Robert set out to make his living in the professional theatre.

There was indeed a bit of money from the Fass estate but Robert, like his father, was not one to exist on a bit of money, scrimping and conserving, and he had inherited more than a keenness for racing — and roulette from his father. He believed in a certain grandeur of style, and the Fass legacy would not support that. Touring was still in its heyday. Companies would set off, probably with productions of plays that were enjoying a successful London run, and tour the provinces for years. There was no question of their ever coming to London — touring was an end itself; thus groups of actors would pass each other at Crewe station on Sundays bound for Blackpool or Margate or Sheffield or some such point in the British Isles where they would stay a week to the delight — or otherwise — of the locals. The system had its own stars and they burned as brightly in Nottingham as did any West End star on Shaftesbury Avenue.

It was on the whole a pleasant life. There was a certain security: once you were engaged in a play the tour would probably last a year or maybe two. It was all pre-booked and you could see your months and days nicely filled, and more importantly you could see the money coming in — maybe not very much if you weren't a star, but it was steady. Actors would write ahead and book digs in theatrical lodgings and their minds were then free. There were matinee days, of course, but most days their time was their own. There was time to visit museums and galleries, cinemas, and other touring companies, and in Robert's case also time to play poker and bridge and visit the local racecourse. It was fortunate that Robert's innate curiosity about people, places and things was constantly stimulated, because he spent nearly ten years on the road. Not as star but as what was termed 'the responsible gentleman' part — a doctor, lawyer, judge — much the kind of part he had played at the Academy, and certainly older than himself.

Robert's first tour lasted almost a year. It was with Russel Thorndike in a play Thorndike had adapted from his own novel, *Dr Syn*. Thorndike gave the kind of performance Robert delighted in watching. He was an actor on the grand scale who towered above everyone on the stage, including Robert, who played the Squire of Dymchurch. Russel Thorndike presented the play in conjunction with Nelson King and it was during this time that Robert met Mrs Nelson King — Nora — a highly respected lady in the profession who, as a general agent, was greatly interested in repertory companies. She visited them all regularly where she found parts for her young hopeful actors and actresses. It was easier to employ actors, of course; girls trying for a stage career still greatly outnumbered the men. In London Mrs Nelson King had a little office in St Martin's Lane at the top of a very steep flight of stairs which was perpetually lined with young people who had come as much for a chat as in hopes of a job. She always made time to listen, to suggest and encourage, and as often as not to lend money. She never took a commission if her clients were hard up — and they generally were. She bought (and always returned unobtrusively) many trinkets that were offered to her when money was needed by the youngsters for the rent or meals. There were other general agents in London who cast tours and reps. It was the practice for young actors to wander from one to the other, waiting in line for their turn, enquiring 'Anything today?' In between they would meet at the ABC for a cup of coffee and discuss prospects or console each other before continuing on the rounds. Mrs Nelson King was a largish lady with an enormous sense of fun and Robert made her laugh a lot. They became immediate friends.

After *Dr Syn,* Robert went off on a tour of *And So to Bed* as Assistant Stage Manager. His duties included making sure the scenery and props were packed up and dispatched to the station on Saturday nights after the show. He managed to leave a good deal of it behind. The practical side of the theatre was not one of his strong points. He preferred dinners, parties, games and conversation. He was in Blackpool touring in *Many Waters* on his 21st birthday. Perhaps it was the party atmosphere of the seaside holiday town with its piers and amusement parks and sideshows that inspired him, or perhaps it was just his general delight in having a good time, but he gave the cast a party for himself and had melons, which were unavailable in Blackpool that month, flown in from London. It was the grand gesture of having them specially delivered in so dramatic a fashion that appealed to him more than the actual melons.

Besides the touring companies in the early 'thirties there were repertory companies where a young actor could be gainfully employed while learning his craft. Robert spent some time at Oxford with the company at the Playhouse. A Wellington contemporary saw him playing a butler in *The Importance of Being Earnest* there and decided that Robert must be up at the university and having a bit of a lark. It was at Oxford that the local newspaper noted 'Robert Morley acted well as the Russian peasant servant' in Shaw's *Arms and the Man.* Also in that season at the Playhouse he acted in J. M. Barrie's one act play, *Half an Hour.* Robert had no difficulty in taking on the parts of middle-aged men and played them with a minimum of make up. His roles at the Festival Theatre repertory in Cambridge were a bit more onerous. Although he was a 'serious' actor in the sense that he had every intention of earning his living that way and indeed of becoming a star, he couldn't really take himself or the theatre with enormous serious*ness*. He has always maintained that it is the function of the actor to entertain the audience and amuse it. Robert thought it terribly amusing when, as Herod in a production of Wilde's *Salome*, he gave a slipping and sliding performance in the blood of John the Baptist. Norman Marshall, guest director at the theatre, was not amused. He felt such clownishness diminished Robert's chances of ever being given a West End role. Robert, although dedicated to becoming a star, preferred to give the impression that he was a gentleman engaged in a bit of a lark, when off the stage — and was totally opposed to pretentiousness on the stage. Norman Marshall confused the two.

It was at Cambridge that Robert met Terence Gray, one of the few people in the theatre he was later to classify as a genius. It is easy to see why his character appealed to Robert. Terence Gray founded the Festival Theatre, yet he was not a professional theatre person in the accepted sense. At the age of thirty he came to the theatre with a reputation as an Egyptologist. He had a wide knowledge of European theatre, he worked immensely hard, his ideas were strikingly original; moreover he had a vivid personality. Although not experienced in the theatre he knew exactly what he wanted to do. His theory of Shakespearian production, for example, sums up his attitudes: 'Fundamentally Shakespeare's characters are always conscious of an audience, they never pretend to be anywhere but on a stage, they welcome and use rather than seek to deny the theatre which is their life. All this I have sought to restore. My actors do not pretend, are not attempting the impossible task, insulting to your intelligence, of persuading you that they are in Bayard's castle, Pomfret or the Tower of London. They are, as they were in Shakespeare's day, frankly on, in or beside a structure which stands as symbol for Bayard's castle, Pomfret or the Tower of London.' Robert has never sought to insult the intelligence of the audience, nor has he ever pretended he was not on a stage when he most palpably was. Terence Gray loved the theatre, he worked hard in it. He brought innovations and experiments to it but never for a moment was it his whole life. When he left the Festival he became a wine grower in France, successfully growing his own vines and producing an excellent vintage. Afterwards he returned to his native Ireland where he turned to breeding horses. Life was very full of a lot of things beside the theatre, wonderful as that could be, yet most successful actors maintain that they are successful because they can't do anything else; if there was a remote possibility they could earn their living in another way they would.

Robert was soon back on tour, this time with Sir Frank Benson. Benson's life's work had been touring Britain bringing Shakespeare to every nook and cranny. His productions were bustling, full of energy and most exciting. Audiences loved him and so did his company. His own performances were athletic — as a student at Oxford he had been noted for athletics and won the three-mile race — but his rendition of the great tragic roles often incomprehensible — he was untrained in speaking Shakespeare and more often than not it showed rather badly. However the stage fights were electrically realistic. He was seventy-five when Robert joined him and had been touring for fifty years. The company called him Pa. He was a charming man, always in debt, but refusing to allow financial insecurity to interfere with his mission of bringing Shakespeare to the people.

After his stint with Benson, touring rather slowed down for Robert. When he was in London out of work he lived in his mother's Chelsea flat (she had returned from the country for a spell), and spent many of his evenings playing bridge or poker with Mrs Nelson King and Tim, her husband, in her house just off St George's Square which she termed Belgravia but was in reality Victoria. Peter Bull, another of her protégés, was often there too when he was out of work in London. She and Robert had gone to see him in Coventry in a play about Nelson called *England Expects,* and Peter remembers his first glimpse of Robert as he stuck his head around the dressing-room door and said: 'That's the worst piece of acting I have ever seen.' Peter agreed with him completely and they became firm friends. In London they played squash together at the RAC but (according to Peter) stopped because Robert wasn't very good at it and he was. They took to playing poker and bridge because Robert was more at home with cards. One night they were playing bridge when Nora's daughter by her first marriage, Meriel Forbes-Robertson, arrived home from her first job at Dundee rep. Meriel was a strikingly pretty girl but rather nervous and shy. Robert was used to shyness — his own mother was painfully nervous — and he soon put her at her ease. They met often at the flat which was always full of good humour and endless card games, as well as a new board game, Monopoly. Peter Bull was rather good at this but had a tendency to be vague, which Robert capitalized on. He would talk incessantly — a stream of stories, imitations and gossip — so that Peter would lose his concentration on the game as he became more and more interested. Then he would discover that he had unwittingly landed on a string of hotels Robert had built while spinning his yarns. To his accusations of cheating, Robert invariably replied: 'Nonsense, that's part of the game.'

Meriel and Robert saw each other on tour, too, when they were in the same town, though they never worked together. One night in Edinburgh they met for supper. It was snowing and very, very late when Robert, walking Meriel back to her digs, decided that maybe he wasn't just keeping an eye on his friend's daughter. Soon afterwards, back in London, he said, 'I think we ought to get married.' He was the first person ever to propose to Meriel, and it never occurred to her that she could say no. It was rather like being asked out to tea — 'What an excellent idea,' she said. 'Yes, please.' She went home and told her mother that Bobbie had asked her to

Daisy Fass, 1902, and

(right) Major Morley

Little Bobbie and Little Cissie

Robert (with beard) in Canon Elliott's Christmas play

Robert at 16

Robert and Peter with Llewellyn Rees separating their matching blazers in California

Robert with Norma Shearer in Marie Antoinette

Keith Campbell, Robert, and Peter Bull in Doctor Knock, *Perranporth, 1939*

marry him and that she had agreed. 'Oh, God!' was her mother's reaction. Robert was fun, and she loved him as she would a son, but she wasn't at all keen to have him for a son-in-law. In a little while he rang Nora himself. He was broke and could she please lend him the money to buy an engagement ring? 'Not bloody likely,' she said. But that wasn't the end of it. The rather vague, conversational engagement continued, as did the bridge evenings.

That year brought Robert a short tour in *Late Night Final*. Never one to be amused by petty backstage gossip and boring theatrical anecdotes, he made up stories to delight Meriel in his letters. He wrote about his expeditions up the Nile beset by crocodiles while she remained safe and secure in her little nest in Victoria — actually he was having tea in Leeds. After that tour he was out of work — but determined not to be idle. Besides he needed money. He was like his father in that he didn't believe in conserving money. Although his sister had managed to invest and save the legacy she had from the family, Robert happily spent his. He got a job selling vacuum cleaners door-to-door — he even demonstrated them and would try out the techniques in the Nelson King flat. He was living with his mother now as she had moved back to Chelsea. She managed to avoid his theatrical friends and her shyness they took for pomposity. Meriel was terrified of her, and Peter Bull rather in awe.

Robert rang Meriel one night and she told him she was about to do a long tour in a play with Robert Donat. He was horrified: 'What about the wedding?' Meriel did the tour. The engagement gradually dissolved, neither party having taken it very seriously in the first place. They still saw each other frequently. 'You'll never really succeed in the theatre,' he told her one day. She arched. 'Why not? I'm never out of work.' Being kind she didn't continue with the obvious 'And you frequently are.' 'That's true,' he replied, 'but you have no ambition. Now, I have enormous ambition and I will succeed.' She didn't believe him. Both Meriel and her mother thought that he would be successful, but not as an actor. He didn't seem to have an actor's mentality. He had an outstanding personality — perhaps he would be a great politician or a writer. He was always full of plots and ideas which he expounded at length most amusingly. He told Meriel an idea he had for a play about the grand people who lived in a house and the servants who looked after them. 'A kind of Upstairs and Below stairs,' he told her. That came later. He called it *Staff Dance,* but first he wrote *Short Story.*

He wasn't getting any work as an actor and his selling techniques were not a huge success, so he got to work on a play. He decided to write it for Marie Tempest, who was a huge star. She was everything a star should be ; she dressed glamorously, she dominated the stage in the kind of light witty roles which Robert loved. She had grace, composure and style as well as technical skill, with beautiful phrasing and diction. In 1925 she had created the role of Judith Bliss in Noel Coward's *Hay Fever* and was enormously popular.

Robert believed in starting at the top — a characteristic most likely inherited from his father. It was an agonizing ordeal as he tried with his first play to capture all the wit and style of Wilde or Lonsdale at their best. Many a night he cried while trying to construct the perfect epigram. Finally it was finished and he sent it to Miss Tempest's manager, Alban Limpus. It came back rather too quickly. Mr Limpus decided that it was the worst play he had ever read and that he wouldn't even show it to Miss Tempest. Disregarding this blow, Robert decided that Mr Limpus wasn't in a position to judge the merits of his play. After all, he wasn't the one who had to face an audience; how could he know what would or would not work on the stage? So he posted *Short Story* directly to Miss Tempest. She could only say no — what would be lost?

He waited for two days — two very long days. Perhaps he had been a bit rash. Was he a playwright or was he an out of work actor? Marie Tempest summoned him to lunch at her grand house in Avenue Road. It could have been a set for one of her comedies. Miss Tempest was seventy that year, yet she was still devastating. There she was as beautifully dressed in real life as on stage. Her hair was tastefully tinted a reddish-gold, and her shoes matched her dress. She wore her famous pearl stud earrings as usual — black in one ear and pink in the other. This overwhelming creature had decided that she would do *Short Story*. There were a few changes needed, of course — changes that would amount to a total rewrite. Robert would have agreed to standing on his head and juggling balls with his feet in a lion's den. Marie Tempest was going to do his play! As she left him to have her usual afternoon nap, her husband wrote him a cheque for £100, which Robert accepted with amazement. All this and money too. It was too much. He sallied forth from the house in a dream and crashed soundly into a post box. Even the pain was glorious. It proved that he was awake and still a playwright. Then it came to rehearsals, and he woke up.

Miss Tempest had some requirements besides the few changes. The play, she said, was to be presented by Tennants, the West End management company then headed by Binkie Beaumont, and it was to be directed by Tyrone Guthrie. Guthrie was still a young man (eight years older than Robert), but he had had great successes both at the Old Vic and in the West End. Robert could not have been more pleased. All that settled, there was the rewriting to start. Originally, *Short Story* was about an actress who had been a failure and who decided to go back to the stage, to the astonishment and later despair of the dramatist who had persuaded her to do so. Marie Tempest wasn't having any of that. 'It is quite inconceivable that the public would accept me as a failure.' Guthrie decided to help Robert with the rewrite. The two men had a lot in common. Guthrie had been born in Tunbridge Wells — a spa town — into a genteel family and had shared the same kind of nursery childhood as Robert, although his family had a bit more stability. He, too, had a very enquiring mind, had been rather frowned upon at school, and tended to be a bit of a rebel. He, too, had been sent to Wellington College when he would rather have been at home, although he had prospered there and won a scholarship to Oxford. Strangely enough he and Robert shared problems with their feet. Robert had hammer toes

35

which could be agony, and Guthrie had gone to the lengths of having a troublesome toe removed while at Wellington. More importantly, they shared an interest and curiosity about nearly everything and everyone. At their first meeting Guthrie thought that Robert was desperately shy; Robert recovered himself though he remained rather in awe of the great man. He was fascinated to see him at work. Guthrie was a disciplinarian. The company had to arrive on time and they had to work very hard, but they also had to delight in their work. At the first sign of boredom Guthrie stopped the rehearsal. There must always be delight, there must always be fun.

Binkie Beaumont looked at the rewritten script and decided on an all-star cast. Not only Marie Tempest but also A. E. Matthews, Sybil Thorndike, Margaret Rutherford, Rex Harrison and Ursula Jeans. The first reading of the play was at His Majesty's Theatre. A. E. Matthews arrived in riding breeches and a Norfolk jacket, riding a bicycle which he propped against the back wall of the stage. Rex Harrison had come by train from Nottingham where he was playing every night, and hovered nervously in the background as the rest of the cast and the director sat round a table waiting for Miss Tempest. She was not late — they were early. She had been on holiday in Sweden. Marie Tempest made her entrance in a grey dress — shoes naturally to match — and carrying a very long, elegant umbrella which she used as a fascinating prop. It was Miss Tempest's custom to rehearse in the evenings. She would arrive in evening dress, and expected the other members of the cast to do so, too. At ten they would go to the Savoy for supper, resuming rehearsals around ten-thirty, and carrying on till midnight. She also rehearsed in the mornings, but in the afternoons the company had to get on with it without her. Rex Harrison caught the train each morning from Nottingham and returned in the afternoon to his role there. The cast remained fairly in awe of Miss Tempest, but not so Mr Guthrie. As Sybil Thorndike remembers: 'Miss Tempest at rehearsal was being very naughty. She would try to make you her slave and if you gave way she despised you and treated you like dirt. One day when she'd been awful Tony [Guthrie] suddenly snapped his fingers and we all stopped. He came striding down the auditorium while we all waited. Then in a loud voice he said, "Miss Tempest! Why are you being such a bitch?" There was an awful silence and we all thought "Poor young man. Such a promising producer and that's the end of it." They looked at each other for a long time and then suddenly that gorgeous smile of hers spread across her face and she said very sweetly, "Very well, Mr Guthrie, shall we go on with the rehearsal?" '

Guthrie had won that round but he wasn't going to capitalize on it. When Rex Harrison had trouble with a bit of stage business, Guthrie called upon Miss Tempest to show him how it was done. She was technically expert and she did the business brilliantly. Peace reigned.

Although she was very keen to have her own way, Marie Tempest was always a professional. At one point she was having trouble learning her lines, and the prompter called out a bit too quickly.

'Did you speak?' she blazed at him.

'Yes, I gave you the line.'

'Are you acting this part or am I?'

'You are trying to and you always dry up on that line.'

There followed an uncomfortably long silence. Then she smiled her devastating smile and said, 'Quite right.'

Short Story was to open at the King's Theatre, Edinburgh, on September 23rd, 1925. Robert travelled up with his mother, in keen anticipation. The local newspapers had done a story about the actor turned playwright and had printed Robert's picture. It was really fame at last. Mother wasn't overly impressed. There was something rather vulgar about publicity. As soon as Robert had settled into his room, carefully hanging his new dinner jacket, the phone rang. 'This is Poodle,' the voice said. Robert nearly fainted. Years before while touring in Scotland he had had a week's flirtation with a dance hall hostess — this same Poodle. On the eve of his triumph he imagined his past coming to haunt him. What if Poodle wanted to meet? His mother would be horrified at the thought of her son consorting with 'that kind of woman'. Robert immediately denied himself. He assured Poodle that he was not Robert Morley the actor but a totally different person, he was Robert Morley the playwright, and he hung up with a sigh of relief. He congratulated himself on being so convincing.

The next night the play went marvellously. Even his mother thought so. Coming out into the foyer his heart sank. There was a beautiful, elegant woman in a magnificent fur coat. It was Poodle. She introduced her husband, a very distinguished, prosperous-looking gentleman. 'Of course you're not the Robert Morley I used to know,' she said. 'If you ever see the other one do tell him from me how happy I am that he's had such a success here tonight and how glad I am that he never forgets his old friends.' Robert felt very foolish — he had been nervous and there was his mother — but none of the many excuses he thought of quite convinced him that he hadn't behaved very badly.

The next morning he gathered the newspapers. The critics were as delighted with *Short Story* as the audience had been: 'Pleasurable expectation was evident in the crowded house and the applause at the close suggested that Miss Tempest has picked a play which is an admirable vehicle for her talents and one which is assured of a long run of success when it goes South.' Some of the other papers said that it wasn't a very original play but that all in all it was a delightful evening in the theatre.

In Manchester the next week audiences and critics loved it — 'a perfect example of the ultra-modern, smart comedy. The plot is slight, the wit caustic and the casting perfect.' In Birmingham and Leeds the reception was just as enthusiastic. The London opening had to be postponed for a few days because Miss Tempest's husband, W. Graham Browne, had been taken ill in Leeds. Although his role would be played by the understudy, Miss Tempest wanted to be with him. *Short Story* opened in London on November 2nd at the Queen's Theatre. The first night audience loved it. It was glittering, bright and witty. The critics found it slight but amusing. On the whole they found Mr Morley a playwright of promise even though this offering was more a vehicle than a play. It ran only three months though in those three months there were some notable occurrences. One night Sybil Thorndike accidentally hit Miss Tempest in the face with a pineapple as the curtain fell. The audience laughed heartily, while Sybil nearly died. However, Miss Tempest acknowledged to the quaking Sybil that she had indeed been standing in the wrong place. It was entirely her fault, she admitted.

Marie Tempest liked *Short Story* very much. In fact she took it on a short tour after it closed in London. The provincial critics were right — it was a very good vehicle for her. Later she told her biographer: 'You know, it's rather amusing the way critics and people talk of ham acting. Now I think that every great actor is ham at some time or other. I think also that the great moments in good plays are often ham. But that's where one's work lies, in covering up the ham.' She then quoted a certain speech she had had in *Short Story* in the role of Georgina: 'The role of the complacent and adoring wife growing old and fat in the country is one which I have played quite long enough. I am tired of it. Simon! When I married you fifteen years ago I was a star. A big star! The most successful actress in London. I could have travelled all over the world and met all the interesting people in the world. I would have known adventure and excitement! Instead I married you and gave up everything else. Don't think I regret it, my dear, I don't. We've been very happy together, but now . . . well, it was never part of my plan to become one of your responsibilities, Simon. "One of your many responsibilities", so now I'm going back. It's not going to be easy, but I'll do it! Give me five years and you'll see!'

'Covering up a moment like that,' she continued, 'and ha! Yes! Making an author's ham seem like kosher.'

Still, *Short Story* had closed rather quickly in London. And Robert was faced with the question: was he an actor or a playwright? And would he ever do either successfully? When in doubt take a holiday — he found a lovely hotel in Cadiz — looked around in the mornings — slept in the afternoons. Barcelona was not to his liking. 'There are 1½ million inhabitants,' he wrote to his mother, 'and 3 million smells — plus incredible rains.' He was sailing at nine for Palma Majorca. That was better. He also stayed in Portugal on that trip. 'I now know everyone in Estoril,' he declared. 'Very social.'

But then home — to what? His friend Peter Bull came up with an interesting proposition.

CHAPTER THREE

THEATRICAL MANAGEMENTS were not exactly banging on Robert's door and he had grown rather weary of banging on theirs, when Peter Bull suggested a novel idea: a summer theatre. Although they were very popular in America, England had never before had one and Peter knew just the place to initiate it. He had been on holiday in Cornwall and in Perranporth, a small village on the north coast, had found a Women's Institute building, the management of which seemed to quite like the idea of a troupe of semi-strolling players taking it over for the season. Peter painted a glorious picture of the sunshine and the bathing and the crowds who would flock to the theatre, and managed to persuade a number of his friends to join him in exchange for room and board and the occasional haircut. At the end of the season they would share out the profits.

Robert had visions of a marvellous gothic house on a cliff with path sloping gently down to the blue warm sea. When he arrived his heart sank. Room and board was to be in 'Mon Repos', a granite edifice of unmitigated gloom with a bootshop on the ground floor, situated in the middle of the village. Peter explained that it was after all a matter of finances — he was not operating with a great deal of capital, but Robert felt that he had been rather misled. Still, he had been promised the lead in *Rope,* to which he was greatly looking forward. Peter had envisaged a true repertory company — doing three or four plays on different nights in the week, thus attracting the same tourists more than once on their fortnight's holiday. Robert was not exactly looking forward to performing three leading parts in the space of a week, but Peter had promised him the roles to get him to come. Now it seemed more like a threat.

However this was the least of the snags involved in the enterprise. The stage they were to occupy measured barely twelve feet across and six and a half feet deep. Roger Furse was appointed art director. He had designed the sets and costumes for some productions at the Gate Theatre in London, and was a friend of Peter's. He was called upon to make something of this rather limited space and it was a mark of his brilliance that he actually achieved the task. Another great problem was that the only exit on the stage was actually the back door to the room and slap in the middle of the back wall. A character leaving the scene presumably for another room landed up in the car park while the audience had trouble suspending its disbelief. Roger overcame this obstacle with a lean-to scenic arrangement, but on wet nights there had to be an umbrella escort to meet exiting performers. While Roger coped with these problems, Robert and the others had to wrap all the ladies' tea cups and saucers in newspaper and pack them away. Somehow this was not how he had envisaged his stage career. Also he had to take his turn at the box office even though maths was not his strong point — and as for allocating seats, well, confusion tended to reign. Overcome with the joy of actually selling a seat he would forget to tick the seating plan. Luckily, because his stage work was so heavy, Robert was excused from selling ice creams to the audience - but other members of the cast did.

The season opened on July 20th, and although the 'house full' signs so beautifully and optimistically prepared were not needed, the auditorium was far from empty. Robert played a middle-aged rather stuffy husband married to a young, flirtatious wife in *To See Ourselves*. To age himself he had applied with a heavy hand a moustache which had a tendency to make him look like a cross walrus. But two

42

nights later was the opening to which he had been looking forward. *Rope* is the story of two undergraduates who murder for kicks, based on the Leopold-Loeb case. They stuff the body into a trunk and proceed arrogantly to entertain the deceased's family to tea which is laid on the trunk. It is a macabre play, and Robert was the poet who tricks the boys into confession. This went down very well. Then, in a much lighter vein two days later came *Springtime for Henry*, a fanciful play for four characters.

As the opening productions settled down into a true repertory there was time for the beach and huge cream teas. Robert even found time to become engaged to a charming local lady who played the piano for the company when music was required. But it was a short-lived romance that soon wilted, as did Robert's spirits. He insisted Peter had promised them food hampers full of goodies from Fortnum and Mason. Peter denied it. Anyway the hampers came not from Fortnum and Mason but from a little shop in Truro. Moreover Robert loathed the last play of the season. It was a Victorian melodrama called *Maria Marten or The Murder in the Red Barn*. He had to play the principal comic part of Tim Bobbin and hated every minute of it, finding it impossible to make funny a part he found distinctly uncomic. He took to throwing sweets at the audience to elicit at least some kind of response — if not laughter perhaps surprise. Every performance was agony.

Robert came to a decision. He was giving up acting. In fact, he gave his make-up box away. The season was over. Everyone was going back to London to work. Could any career be more ludicrous than that of pretending to be someone else every night on a stage? Was that really something a grown man should be doing with his time? His mother had been right. Acting was not a profession. It was childish and unfulfilling and undignified. And it was especially ridiculous if no one wanted you. The Perranporth profits were shared out. Robert had £15. He hired a cottage with Peter Bull and Pauline Letts, who was also in the company. He would have a real holiday before returning to London and deciding what he would do with his life. After all, it wasn't too late to start again. He was barely turned twenty-eight. The world was open to him — and he certainly wasn't going to waste his time in the theatre. He'd been working eight years and no one had recognized his star potential. And he'd always known that if he couldn't be a star he wouldn't be anything. He'd written a play that had had an all-star cast and how long had it run? A few months. It was a fickle profession and he would have no more to do with it.

Unless, of course, someone asked. Norman Marshall, whom Robert had worked under at the Festival Theatre, Cambridge, was at this time running the Gate Theatre in London. About a year and a half before he had wanted to produce an English version of Maurice Rostand's play about Oscar Wilde. Lord Alfred Douglas objected very strongly. He called Rostand's play 'a travesty of the truth and a deliberate misrepresentation of well-known facts. It is sufficient to point out that the whole idea of Rostand's play was based on the false assumption that I had never seen or spoken to Oscar Wilde again after he came out of prison. I saw him constantly (often daily for months at a time), I continually supplied him with money and when he died I paid for his funeral and was the principal mourner at the church of Saint Germain des Prés and at the cemetery at Bagneux.' Such arguments as Lord Alfred Douglas put forward, backed up of course by the fact that legally he could object to his representation on stage, convinced Marshall that he had better abandon the idea for the time. Later he was delighted when Sewell Stokes and his brother, Leslie, gave him a play they had written about Wilde. First things first. Marshall and Stokes hurried down to Lord Alfred Douglas' home in Hove clutching the manuscript. Lord Alfred approved. He agreed at once to its performance, with a few minor alterations in the text.

They had been rehearsing for about a fortnight when Gerald Cooper, who was playing Wilde, decided he couldn't continue. He was just not suited to the part and asked to be released. The Stokeses had had an actor called Frank Pettingell in mind when they wrote the play, but unfortunately he wasn't available. What were they going to do? They had a play, a production even, and no one to play the lead. Robert Morley's name was suggested. Norman Marshall wasn't exactly elated with the proposal. He remembered Herod: 'In his early days Robert Morley was as unpromising an actor as I have ever seen. Although he had been on the stage for eight years he had never played a part in London. But he bore a striking resemblance to Wilde so at least it seemed worth while hearing him read a scene.' He called Robert and gave him the play. Robert took it off to Rules, one of his favourite restaurants — and one he could ill afford — read it over lunch while Norman and Sewell and the production waited. Then Norman spotted him walking down Villiers Street toward the theatre. 'Well, there's your Oscar,' he said to Sewell.

Sewell had never met Robert nor indeed seen him. But his reputation as a provincial actor not capable of a West End part had preceded him. Sewell thought Robert would be delighted. He had been such a flop as an actor he was about to give up the theatre and now he was being given this marvellous opportunity. Robert came in wearing a black felt hat with an enormous brim and smoking an equally enormous cigar, carrying the play in his hand. Sewell waited for the gushing gratitude.

'I've read your little play,' Robert told him. 'It won't quite do, will it, dear, but I think we can get it right.'

Sewell was speechless. This did seem arrogance — and Robert hadn't even read for the part. But when he did both Sewell and Norman realized that he was ideal. And Sewell soon discovered that Robert wasn't being grand - just honest. As Sewell said later, 'He did get the play right. Where one had ended an act one way Robert ended it another and he was in fact terribly valuable.'

There was another problem with rehearsals, though, besides the rewriting. Villiers Street was lined with amusement arcades full of pin ball machines and various penny-in-the-slot games. It was impossible to get Robert past them. Sewell was often deputed to go and almost physically drag him back to the theatre. Gambling has always had a rather relaxing effect on Robert and after all he was in need of relaxation. He was about to face his first major appearance on a London stage. Would he muff it? The bells and clatter of the pin table, the lights declaring him a winner — they were soothing.

Oscar Wilde opened at the Gate Theatre Studio on September 29th, 1936, a year and a week since Robert had seen the opening of *Short Story*. The Lord Chamberlain still deemed the subject of homosexuality on stage objectionable, and therefore a club theatre was necessary. The critics rather reflected the prevailing moral climate in their reviews. Though Matthew Norgate spoke of it as being handled with 'discretion and good taste', others spoke of 'unsavoury details' or 'an unpleasant taste in the mouth'. Yet the consensus was that Robert Morley was 'very good indeed in the chief part'. With amazing prescience one reviewer noted 'Mr Robert Morley in the leading part manages to look far more like Oscar Wilde than Miss Norma Shearer, though the resemblance is there.' The *Saturday Review* enthused whole-heartedly: 'I cannot speak too highly of Mr Robert Morley's unforgettable performance as Wilde. His was no easy task but he carried it out with a delicacy and yet a forcefulness which I could not over praise if I tried. I have added Mr Morley to my collection of actors who really know how to act.' And the public came. There were full houses for the entire six week run. Robert had done it, and he had proved what he had always maintained, that given a star part he could not only be a star but he could act as well. However, *Oscar Wilde* was scheduled as a limited run, and after six weeks he was again without work.

Very quickly he had two offers. One was from Tyrone Guthrie who was directing a Shakespeare season at the Old Vic. Laurence Olivier was to play Hamlet and Guthrie wondered if Robert would play the King. Yes, please, was Robert's reaction. He admired Guthrie and although it wasn't the star part it was a showy one. At the same time Robert Kane was producing a film at Denham *Under the Red Robe* — a swashbuckler to star Conrad Veight and Annabella, the French film star. He wanted Robert to be dialogue coach and also to have a small part. Easy — he could do that in the daytime and give his Claudius at night at the Old Vic. But Kane insisted upon testing even the smallest parts. After Robert's screen test, he decided he wanted him for one of the main parts. This he would not be able to do and carry on at the Old Vic. The American producer was offering a lot of money. Guthrie released Robert and he set out to conquer the screen. The director was to be Victor Sjostrom, a distinguished Swedish filmmaker who had been successful in Hollywood as Victor Seastrom. With German and American stars and a Swedish director it wasn't surprising that Kane wanted a dialogue coach. As Robert remembers: 'My first task was to get one of my fellow actors to say the curious line, "The Cardinal's down, he'll hang no more poor fellows." When he'd said it a couple of times, the director called me over and asked me to tell him to say it differently. And when I asked him what change he desired, he said, "Well, I want some sort of inflection." "But what sort of inflection?" I said and he said, "More like this: The Cardinal's down he'll hang no more . . . poor fellows." I pointed out to him that so far as I could see there was no inflection there, only a slight pause, which wasn't at all the same thing. Anyway I tried again and finally the scene was shot, not, I thought entirely to Mr Seastrom's satisfaction. As I was leaving at the end of the day, someone came up to me and whispered, "Never, *never* argue with the director on the set." At home that evening I got a call from the studio. It was to say that I had been sacked. I wasn't even asked to play my original part.' Robert cried. Two jobs gone at a stroke. And it was all Mr Kane's fault. He sat down to write him a bitter letter which went: 'How could you take an actor of sensitivity, place him in a costume he disliked and wig he distrusted and then expect him to perform . . . ' and much more in a similar vein. Hayes Hunter, who was then

47

Robert's agent, wouldn't let him send it. Then Kane sent him a cheque for £200. Perhaps life wasn't so bad after all. He had been very good as Wilde; he had proved he could act, and he had some money. He wasn't going to go back to the provinces: that part of his life was over, though he could already look back upon it with nostalgia. He decided to write a play about touring. It would be good for Perranporth.

The Repertory Players performed plays on Sunday nights at the Strand Theatre in London for other actors to watch, and, more importantly, for agents and producers to view the out-of-work talent. In May of 1937 they produced Jules Eckert Goodman's comedy *The Great Romancer* about the life of Alexandre Dumas the elder, the author of *The Three Musketeers*. Charles Lefaux gave Robert the lead, and he was back on the stage where he had begun as a silent pirate. The more dedicated critics usually came to these productions, and on that Sunday night they were ecstatic. W. A. Darlington wrote: 'It is a lively, witty character sketch of that strong, flamboyant personality and prolific writer, Alexandre Dumas the elder. It brings out the immense vitality and gusto of the man and is so theatrically effective that it justifies any liberties that have been taken with historical accuracy. The part is magnificently played by Robert Morley.' Others wrote with the same sparkling enthusiasm. Bronson Albery decided to put it on in the West End at the New Theatre. Robert was very keen on the part. It gave him the best entrance he'd ever had: for the first ten munutes everyone on stage keeps talking about him and asking where he is, then he enters, hair frizzed, small moustache and a sprinkling of hair under his lip, carrying a rabbit on a chafing dish and proclaiming: 'A rabbit stuffed in its own fur, I defy you to taste the skin!' It was a vivid, noisy, flamboyant play.

The first night audience was vociferous, and one of the critics reported: 'He [Robert] was cheered and recalled again and again at the end, and the audience did not cease to applaud until he had made a modest (and almost inaudible) speech of thanks.' The next morning he was pronounced 'A

Stage Star Overnight' by all the papers. 'With what an assured sweep of swagger he endows the hero! How cleverly he manages his voice so as to give a continuous air of impromptu wit to his conversation! How delicately he introduces the little touches of sentiment,' raved the *Evening News*. Robert worried a bit about his voice — would it stand the strain of such a long and energetic role? — but otherwise he was stunned with delight. The newspapers descended on him and he gave interview after interview. Yes, he had been intended for the diplomatic service — yes, he had been acting for seven years — yes, he was the author of *Short Story* — yes, he had just written a play for Peter Bull to produce at Perranporth. And yes, he was absolutely delighted with his success and, of course, a little humble. He was exhausted by it all. After the two shows on Saturday, Coral Browne, a vibrant brunette from Australia who played one of Dumas' romances, wanted him to accompany her to Brighton to celebrate. She had not been on stage almost continuously, and Robert's part was as long as Hamlet and in many ways trickier. Sewell Stokes was backstage congratulating Robert on his success. 'What can I do,' he wailed, 'I'm so tired.' Sewell reluctantly agreed to accompany them as far as Victoria. In the taxi Coral was bright and vivacious while Robert fell sound asleep. So much for the treat — and the exciting life of a West End star.

On Monday night the auditorium wasn't full — far from it. Tuesday there were even fewer people. After all those marvellous reviews and the fantastic publicity, Robert couldn't believe it. They hung on and waited for the audience to build. It fell off. After twelve days *The Great Romancer* closed. No one connnected with it could understand what had happened. Why had no one come? Bronson Albery, who had lost a good deal of money, said: 'In the world of the theatre there are occasionally things for which one can't account at all.' And the desolate star told the *Express* reporter, 'I'd rather not say anything about the play. It just didn't run. It had every chance, but it just didn't attract.'

Robert hadn't really planned to go to Perranporth that

summer. His contribution to the season was to have been a new play he had written while staying at Beachy Head with an aunt. He thought he would be running on at the New. However, there were plans to take *Oscar Wilde* to New York in the autumn and until then he might as well join Peter Bull again. Besides he could direct the premiere of *Goodness How Sad* himself. This time the Cornish season was better organized. There was a proper house and housekeeper and a full-time box office lady. The stage at the Women's Institute had been expanded a bit and there was a proper room built on at the back which obviated the need for the umbrella guard. Besides this, Peter had the audience in mind as well as the actors and had acquired some second-hand deck chairs, which would be more comfortable than the straight-backed kitchen variety they had been using. But a number of them looked suspect. He feared a collapse and deputed Robert to test them by sitting in them and rocking with laughter, as the audience was expected to do. If they withstood Robert's weight they were passed as acceptable.

Goodness How Sad had been written for the company. Peter Bull, Frith Banbury, Pauline Letts and Judith Furse all had parts tailor-made. The company ran banners across the road proclaiming a world premiere, the local paper never stopped writing about it, and even some London papers turned up. It opened on July 26th and everyone, players and audiences alike, were delighted with it. They began plans to take it to London. Meanwhile there was the Perranporth season to get on with and *The Importance of Being Earnest* soon entered the repertory. That August, *Under the Red Robe* was released. How delighted Robert must have been that he had been sacked from it when he read the reviews. On the 20th, *The Spectator* published this one: 'This film, from its awkwardly gesticulating cloak and sword extras to its mixture of real and patently bogus exterior scenes, is one of the most pathetic pieces of nonsense that has ever emerged from a British studio.' It was Victor Seastrom's last film as a director.

Robert had to leave his part of Chasuble in *The Importance of Being Earnest* to Peter Bull and hurry off to London for rehearsals at the Old Vic. Undeterred by Robert's failure to play in *Hamlet,* Tyrone Guthrie had invited him to play Henry Higgins to Diana Wynyard's Eliza in *Pygmalion.* To be playing Shaw at the Old Vic was an honour and knowing that it was a limited run, he wouldn't have to worry about the abrupt closure he had experienced before. This production was happily a success. The critics beamed approval yet again, but this time in a more dignified way: 'Mr Morley has the right Shavian manner, eloquent but off-hand, for Higgins, and presents the mannerless pedant very justly' from the *Evening News,* and Lionel Hale in the *News Chronicle* said: 'I do not wish to see a better Higgins.'

At last the players in Perranporth were getting food hampers from Fortnum and Mason — Robert was sending them. Higgins took away the bitter taste left by the unpredictable failure of Dumas — and moreover there were inklings from Hollywood.

Hunt Stromberg was producing an MGM epic. They had wanted Charles Laughton to play the part of King Louis XVI of France. Stromberg had come to London once again to try to persuade Charles Laughton to go to America for this film — it had been in preparation for five years, and was going to be a very big picture. But Laughton had massive tax problems that prevented his leaving the country. The answer was no. Who, Stromberg wondered, was this Robert Morley the newspapers were full of? He bought himself a ticket and was in the audience one of those twelve nights when Robert played Dumas for all he was worth. Stromberg was more than a little impressed, not only by the bravura of the performance and the intensity with which Robert ate an apple, but also, underneath that moustache, he detected a resemblance to the French king. Would Robert be interested? Tests were made in England. Fine. But the important consideration was Norma Shearer, who would star. Would she approve of him? Could he come to Hollywood to make a test? Hayes Hunter, Robert's agent, was sent off to negotiate terms with MGM in London. Hayes was always pleased to negotiate for Robert. 'You see,' he told a friend, 'he doesn't really want to work.' That wasn't strictly true, but it showed what a good actor Robert was. He was convinced that if his agent thought he had nothing to lose he would hold out for the best possible terms. And this is what happened in most cases. Hunter wasn't afraid of losing Robert a job. Robert got an advance from MGM, and went off to Simpsons to buy a new overcoat for the journey. While he was there he saw a rather smart blue blazer — just the thing for fashionable Hollywood — and he bought that too.

Then came the part he dreaded. Saying goodbye to his mother — that was never an easy task in the best of times. Poor, poor Daisy always looked on the gloomy side. She still firmly believed that acting was not the right profession for her son. It was insecure and rather silly. She always hoped he would give it up and go into the government or business. And she was always convinced that any separation was going to be final. Robert, though he did not live in her pocket, often visited her and sometimes stayed with her. Going all the way to America — and the west coast to boot! Something was bound to happen — his ship would sink — his train would crash — or else she would die of a heart attack before he returned. But mainly she feared that one of them would die before her only son had done something she could feel proud to tell her friends about. They would never meet again, she was sure of it. This was it — the final goodbye. Even Robert was rather shaken by her determination that this was forever, but he managed to overcome it and excitedly boarded the *Bremen* bound for New York.

CHAPTER FOUR

ROBERT WAS NOT YET THIRTY. Here he was, mid-Atlantic and heading for Hollywood. It wasn't really easy to believe. Perhaps Norma Shearer wouldn't like him. After all, it was her picture and practically her town. Stars were all important in Hollywood. Laurence Olivier had been sent packing by Greta Garbo not long before. Still, whatever the outcome Robert decided to make the most of the trip. Llewellyn Rees was in New York stage-managing a play called *George and Margaret*. Llewellyn had been at the Royal Academy with Robert and more recently in *Oscar Wilde*. There was no point in being alone in New York. He would have to brave Hollywood alone, and that was enough. Robert decided to cable Llewellyn but he waited till he was close to the coast because he thought it would be cheaper that way. 'Find me a hotel for the night,' he bid his friend, who duly dropped everything, fixed a room in the hotel he was staying at and went off to meet the ship. Robert was on deck as the ship pulled into New York harbour. It was cold but he had his new overcoat and he wasn't going to miss the Statue of Liberty and the glorious sky-line, so familiar from films. There was a tricky moment when he came to immigration, though. From his medical report the official decided that he couldn't be allowed into the country. One of Robert's eyes was defective. 'What sort of work do you do?' the customs man asked him. 'I'm an actor,' Robert told him, and the man stamped his passport. 'An actor. I guess they're blind half the time anyway, so it won't really matter if you're half blind all the time.'

'Now, Lulu,' he told Llewellyn who was patiently waiting at the dockside, 'You must show me everything.' It turned out that Robert had two rooms reserved in the city for the night because his agent had also booked him one. In the end he used neither of them as he dragged Llewellyn from one club to another through the night. He wasn't going to miss anything. Llewellyn complained loudly. He had to take an understudy rehearsal in the morning. 'Nonsense,' Robert kept exclaiming as they visited yet another club. The next morning Robert flew to California, promising to write. To Llewellyn as he dragged himself to the rehearsal it sounded more like a threat.

Irving Thalberg had conceived the idea of filming *Marie Antoinette*. Thalberg, together with Louis B. Mayer, had practically invented Hollywood and the big studio system, which kept American movies on the top of the world's charts for a generation. But besides the system, Thalberg cared about quality in every aspect of film-making from the notion right through the script to the lighting and costumes. He had been responsible for such blockbusters as *Ben-Hur*, *The Broadway Melody*, *The Barretts of Wimpole Street*, *A Night at the Opera*, *The Good Earth* and *Camille*. *Marie Antoinette* was to be a sweeping survey of the French revolution, but most of all it was to be a vehicle for his adored wife Norma Shearer.

At first meeting she reminded Robert very much of Marie Tempest, both in size and temperament as well as in determination and professionalism. The tests went well, and Robert was given the part of Louis XVI of France. He was also given a flat, a Filipino houseboy called Sammy who cooked exquisitely, a Swedish chauffeur who had illusions of grandeur and wanted to be Robert's secretary, and Hollywood's first portable dressing-room. All the more recent ones were being used by the female stars on the film so they dug up the old one from the depths of the prop department. It was small and box-like but had been originally built for Mabel Normand. She had hammered a horseshoe on the door. It was still there although rusted from its original gilt, and Marie Dressler's rocking chair was still inside. Robert was delighted with it all — except the chauffeur. *George and Margaret* had closed in New York, so Robert wrote to Llewellyn. Would he please come out and be his secretary-cum-driver? Llewellyn moved into the flat in Westwood Village and began the task of organizing Robert.

Sidney Franklin, a careful, slow, meticulous director who had made *The Good Earth,* was originally scheduled to direct this epic. At the eleventh hour he was replaced by W. S. (Woody) Van Dyke, known in the business as 'One Take Van Dyke' and noted mainly for directing *Tarzan* and *The Thin Man* series. Speculation was high in the community about this replacement. It was well known that Miss Shearer was accustomed to about twenty-five takes on each scene. Was head office trying to sabotage the film? The first shot was to be of Miss Shearer making an entrance down a grand staircase — the set a full copy of Versailles. Bewigged and massively costumed she stood at the top, then slowly made her descent. 'All right, in the can,' he said. 'Over to the next set.' Miss Shearer was astounded. 'Oh,' she said. 'Aren't we going to do it again?' Van Dyke looked at her and said most pleasantly, 'There is only one way to walk down a flight of stairs.' The assembled crew and cast waited for an explosion. It didn't come, and Van Dyke kept to his method of working right through the film. He told the press he saw no difference between directing a picture like this and *The Thin Man* except that in the latter he had no costumes and wigs to cope with. And what costumes. One of Miss Shearer's dresses had a wheelbase of eight feet, was supported by forty pounds of steel framework and eleven muslin petticoats. It was made of silver cloth, festooned with diamonds and pearls, spattered with sequins and peppered with pearls. On her head in one scene she wore a white wig covered with a couple of hundred curls, half a dozen aigrette feathers, some silver stars, some golden suns and some diamond bangles. And all her jewellery was real, not paste.

Robert's costumes were no less splendid. For his wedding scene he wore a blue velvet cape with a six foot train — not only was it completely covered in gold hand embroidery but it was also completely lined in ermine. It was an exact copy of the royal original.

Robert's first day on the set was the storming of the palace scene. All he had to do was stand at the top of the stairs and register alarm. From eight in the morning a huge number of very tough-looking Hollywood extras behaved like the mob at Versailles. Even Van Dyke needed more than one take with this number of people involved. Filming always finished at five o'clock on his set. At ten to five the biggest of the extras, a burly gentleman, was deputed by the others to approach Robert. 'Say, Captain,' the man rasped, 'muff this shot, will you?' The extras wanted to be called back in the morning as they were paid by the day. Robert was so terrified of reprisals that his reaction to the mob on film was very nearly genuine.

By this time Peter Bull had joined Llewellyn and Robert in Westwood Village. He took the duplex next door. Monopoly had found its way to Hollywood and it was a nice change playing on the American board where instead of Park Lane and Mayfair there was Boardwalk and other Atlantic City landmarks. The producers had seen Peter's picture in *Spotlight,* the publication that lists available actors, and thought he looked rather like a tough all-in wrestler — just right for the part of the blacksmith. Robert and Llewellyn met him off the plane, Robert feeling very much the Californian in his smart blue blazer. It had been the perfect buy. And there from the plane stepped Peter, wearing the identical blazer. He, too, had been to Simpsons. Robert wasn't pleased. They agreed to wear them on alternate days.

Most of Peter's scenes were with Robert, except his death scene. Here, unfortunately, 'One Take' Van Dyke did not live up to his name. The mob attacked the blacksmith, who fell, blood pouring from his mouth. To achieve this effect Peter had a sachet of chocolate clenched between his teeth.

One hard bite and it poured forth. Take after take, bite after bite — he was off chocolate for months. Robert advised him not to complain. 'That is what they are paying you for.'

This was the period when Hollywood was at its most Hollywood. A three-piece orchestra played chamber music on the set. Robert was invited to parties where he met all the people he'd never actually thought of as being real. Fred Astaire, Jeanette MacDonald, Joan Crawford. Disappointment set in. They all seemed rather small. He was too used to their magnified image projected on the silver screen. But the famous Hollywood premieres were every bit as grand and bizarre as he had anticipated. At the Cathay Circle Theatre there was the world premiere of Disney's *Snow White and the Seven Dwarfs*. They booked two seats, and Robert and Llewellyn put on dinner jackets and set off. A couple of miles from the theatre they were stopped by a cordon of police, and then allowed to continue as they were in evening dress. Searchlights scanned the sky, tiers of people lined the pavements watching the stars arrive. Robert walked on the red carpet behind Carole Lombard, and there was Charlie Chaplin, and next to him in the cinema, Marlene Dietrich. Shirley Temple arrived with seven real dwarfs.

If the eyes of the world were on Hollywood, Hollywood's eyes were only on itself. The papers were full of news about the industry, a good deal of it made up by press agents hired by the studios specifically for this purpose. By and large no one thought or talked about much except the films. And amusement came from seeing others and being seen at parties and, of course, from the films themselves. One night Robert heard there was the premiere of an MGM film down the road, so he and Peter, being employed by the company, thought they ought to attend. They dressed up and set off. The inevitable man with the microphone welcomed them outside the cinema and asked them some questions about *Marie Antoinette* 'for our listeners at home'. He told them how wonderful it was to see them and wished them great success with the film. The audience lined up on the pavement applauded loudly as Peter and Robert waved and smiled their way to the door of the cinema — where they were refused admission. 'But,' Peter remonstrated, 'this is the star of *Marie Antoinette*. This is Louis XVI.' 'You haven't got tickets and it is all sold out,' they were told firmly. So they sneaked sheepishly back past the crowds and returned home to play Monopoly.

But even Monopoly palled after a while, and they went in search of bigger game. There was a ship called the Rex moored off Santa Monica just outside the three-mile limit. Down in the harbour was a boat that advertized 'trips round the bay'; in actual fact it just shot straight off to the Rex. On board were all the games Robert could wish for — poker, black jack, roulette. Llewellyn insisted they were crooked, but Robert couldn't be dissuaded. In Palm Springs he had found a house in the middle of nowhere also dedicated to gambling. Dollar after dollar was lost at the roulette table. Putting his hand in his pocket for more he pulled out a postcard he had bought that afternoon. It was a picture of a little prairie donkey and underneath was printed 'Little denizen of the desert'. Robert took it as an omen and went home — but he wasn't usually so easily discouraged. Finally Llewellyn decided to take complete control of Robert's income and doled out money to him only in amounts he could afford to lose.

By early March the entire film was in the can except for the guillotine scenes. Van Dyke decided to give the cast a rest and the film cutters a chance to catch up. He called a two-week halt to shooting. Norma Shearer went off to Sun Valley, Idaho. Robert and Peter set off in their studio car with Llewellyn at the wheel to explore.

To keep themselves awake while driving across the endless desert in search of the Grand Canyon they played word games — Twenty Questions, Who Am I? and even I Spy. It wasn't the sophisticated life Robert had envisaged. Occasionally, to pass the time they would ask him to sell them a vacuum cleaner. 'Madam,' he would begin, 'do you have young children in the house? Well, let me tell you

58

that the cleaner you have been using is most unhealthy — it actually blows dust out!'

They were suitably impressed with the Grand Canyon and the Boulder Dam. Not so with Salt Lake City. Robert pronounced it the ugliest, most boring place he'd ever been, and couldn't understand why Llewellyn had driven them there. Poor Llewellyn was about to protest that it had been Robert's idea when Peter chimed in that he, too, hated it, and besides it was his birthday. 'What do you want for a present?' Robert asked. 'I want to get out of Salt Lake City,' Peter replied, so they piled back into the car and headed across the salt desert towards Las Vegas.

Las Vegas in those days was not yet the glittering playground it has become — in fact it was a fairly tatty town, but paradise compared to Salt Lake City where everything was forbidden. From Las Vegas it was on to Reno, Nevada where nothing was forbidden. Banners hanging over the streets proclaimed Reno 'the greatest little town in the world'. The cowboys who roamed the streets looked straight out of central casting. This was the place to get married in a hurry or divorced just as quickly. In the hotel lobby there hung a list of available co-respondents for those seeking divorce and in need of collaboration. The brothels had cubicles with the ladies' names on the door, and everywhere there loomed the one armed bandit, the fruit machine. To add to all this pleasure they were snowed in. No one could leave Reno. Llewellyn despaired and cut their pocket money down to five dollars a day for the duration. Robert tried everything to get more. He begged, he cajoled, he finally threatened. He was going to sack Llewellyn. Lulu just smiled and tightened the purse. One day Robert turned on Peter who was down to his last nickel. Robert wanted it. He knew he could get the jackpot. 'If you don't give me that nickel I shall take away the rights to *Goodness How Sad*. I won't allow you to produce it in London.' Peter thought about it for a moment. He bounced the nickel in his hand while Robert glowered at him. Then he firmly put the nickel into the slot himself, pulled the handle — and won the jackpot.

Finally, to Llewellyn's relief he was told that if he put chains on his tyres he could get through the pass to Sacramento. He hurried. One more argument like the last one and they might come to blows. And so back to Hollywood. Robert had a bit of work left on the film and Peter had to stay on in case any re-takes were needed. He was anxious to get back to England. There was the Perranporth season to organize. He and Robert had spent a good deal of time trying to lure some of the Hollywood stars to Cornwall. Although a number of papers reported that Joan Crawford and her current husband Franchot Tone were going to make the trip, nothing ever came of it. Besides, Peter, thanks to Llewellyn keeping a tight rein on the money, had saved enough to bring *Goodness How Sad* to London. There was plenty to do at home and not much to do in Hollywood. Finally he was released. He planned to take the scenic route back to New York and travel by train. Robert went off to the studios and Llewellyn drove Peter to the station, staying to wave him goodbye. As Peter leaned out of the window, relieved to be getting off at last, he saw Robert hurrying towards him. 'Stop,' Robert called. 'You're needed for re-takes.' For one horrible moment Peter believed him. Then Robert laughed at his white, bloodless face and wished him a good trip as the train pulled out. He was free to wear his blue blazer every day now if he wished to.

In June the film was finished. It had taken six months' filming, four years' researching and cost nearly two million dollars — a lot of money to lavish on a production in 1938. Robert was invited to the first screening of it in the studio theatre: 'I sat with Mayer and Shearer and behind us sat the executive might of the studio, accompanied by their secretaries and/or mistresses. The picture seemed to last forever and halfway through I began to despair not only of my own performance but of Shearer's and everyone else's. At last it was over and the lights came on. There was a long silence. No one said a word, although some of the secretaries ostentatiously snuffled into their handkerchiefs. From behind someone clapped three times, then stopped. "After a film like that, LB, what is there to say?" was the only comment I heard. For some reason I was convinced that Mayer was going to ask me what I thought and that I would have to tell him. I got up and scrambled over his feet and fled for the exit. I walked out of the theatre and off the lot and along Culver City Boulevard, convinced that every car that overtook me contained some studio official deputed to capture me and bring me back to where Mr Mayer was now sitting on his throne, waiting to ask the fatal question. An hour later, I was still marching down the endless, unpaved street, but this time frightened lest I should encounter one of the packs of wild dogs that they said were often on the prowl in those parts. I got home about five in the morning.'

Llewellyn had gone back to England shortly after Peter and now that the film was finished Robert began packing up too. The world premiere was to be held at the Cathay Circle on July 8th, but Robert wasn't staying for it. July, after all, was the time to be in Cornwall. Besides, he had to convince his mother that he was still alive before heading back to New York in the autumn. He left on June 19th. Louis Mayer invited him to lunch at the palatial executive dining-room. It was practically Versailles all over again. He told Robert he had great faith in him as a film actor, that he very much wanted to find other pictures for him. 'When you've finished your play just let me know and we'll have a picture for you. In the meantime, if any other studio makes you an offer, all I ask is that you'll give me a chance to match it.' So Robert left happy, secure in the knowledge that he was wanted, in spite of what he thought about his own performance. Nothing would induce him to remain for the premiere. He was sure the film would be an incredible anti-climax and that his own performance in particular would draw jeers. He could hear the audience laughing at his bumbling king.

Although Robert couldn't bring himself to attend the premiere, according to Hedda Hopper everyone else did and they could have held it at the Hollywood Bowl. More than 25,000 spectators began arriving at noon just to get a good place to watch the stars arriving. The temporary grandstand

61

held 4000 spectators. The street leading to the theatre was filled with flowers and shrubs and even a fountain — a replica of the garden at Versailles, while under the canopy raised to shield the stars as they walked to the theatre was a recreation of the Garden of the Petit Trianon. A thirty-piece orchestra, accompanying a chorus of twenty-four voices, entertained the spectators. Norma Shearer arrived with Tyrone Power, Louis Mayer and Helen Hayes. And child star Freddie Bartholomew had his first date that night — with Judy Garland. After the film Mayer entertained 600 guests to a party at the Trocadero where it was reported that Norma Shearer danced the night away with Jimmy Stewart. And what about the film? After all that, who in Hollywood would dare not praise it? 'Triumphing in both glamour and realism,' the *Los Angeles Times* reported. 'The screen's finest artistry,' said *Variety*. 'This picture is Hollywood at its best' wrote the *Los Angeles Evening Herald and Express*. And Robert's performance was tipped to win an Oscar. 'Robert Morley is an illuminative influence. His character undergoes the most remarkable development and he makes this patent at every stage.' And *Variety* raved: 'As fine and commanding a piece of acting as the screen has ever seen is Robert Morley's thoughtful and supremely pathetic portrayal of the young king... His every scene is excellent, his final scene with his family a masterpiece.' Hedda Hopper couldn't resist a snide reference to Charles Laughton, who had turned the part down: 'A greater star who can do anything Laughton can and a lot more.'

But Peter Bull was not to be seen in the film. He ended up on the cutting room floor. His theory for the excision was that everyone was so afraid Robert would steal the picture completely that they cut a good number of his scenes — and those just happened to be Peter's too.

The film went to New York in August. That city's press were not as gushingly enthusiastic, finding it too long and too glamorous, but they did tend to agree about Robert's performance: 'One of the finest, most artistic and most original characterizations seen on the screen in some years.'

62

Robert was pleased but not convinced.

Meanwhile at Perranporth things were getting better and better. This year Peter had taken two houses, more to Robert's liking, and had bought some proper tip-up plush seats from an old cinema in Manchester. Roger Furse couldn't make it, but most of the regulars were there together with Pamela Brown. Sewell Stokes was a frequent visitor. This season they managed their now mandatory premiere with a new play by Noel Langley whom they had met in Hollywood where he was working on film scripts including *The Wizard of Oz*. Over Cornish cream teas Robert and Peter regaled the company with stories of Hollywood — already disagreeing violently with each other over details. And all the time in the background plans were being made. Peter was going to open *Goodness How Sad* in the autumn in London and Robert was going back to America, this time to Broadway with *Oscar Wilde*. There was his mother to face again. He pointed out to her that neither of them had died while they were separated by the Atlantic in the winter — but she remained convinced that it would happen this time.

CHAPTER FIVE

GILBERT MILLER, THE LEADING NEW YORK theatrical producing manager, had wanted to produce *Oscar Wilde* in New York after Christmas in early 1938, but Robert was busy with MGM who had indeed promised that the English management of the play would be compensated for the delay. The money never came. Still it was now autumn and the play was going on. Europe was in turmoil and with Germany mobilizing and Chamberlain dashing back and forth from one country to the next trying to bring accord, Robert was pleased to be getting away from the tension, but slightly worried that this time his mother's forebodings might have some basis. He took a two-roomed flat at the St. Moritz. It overlooked the Park and had a small kitchen which he used solely for making coffee and beef tea. He didn't spend much time in it. Downstairs was Rumplemeyers and the best hot fudge sundaes in town. New York was lively and a great relief from the gloom of Europe. Perhaps he'd stay. The papers were full of sensational news about the crisis in Europe and although Robert suspected most of it was misinformed and that Chamberlain was just playing to the gallery, he wrote to his mother that she ought to consider emigrating.

Marie Antoinette had just opened in New York and wherever Robert went people asked for autographs. At first he quite enjoyed it, but after a while he got rather fed up with it. He found himself constantly involved in aimless

Robert and Joan on their wedding day and (right) Fairmans

As Leslie Stuart in You Will Remember

With Emlyn Williams, You Will Remember

George Bernard Shaw, Robert and Gabriel Pascal discussing Major Barbara

Robert, Mitzi, Sheridan, Joan, 1942

A recalcitrant Fox in The Young Pitt

conversations with strangers. Now, he would have quite enjoyed this — besides gambling, having aimless conversations with strangers is one of his favourite ways of passing the time — but he did have a play to get on with. There was casting and lots of fittings for his costumes, and he was rather nervous. September progressed and the news from Britain was getting more hysterical. New York papers reported that beneath Hyde Park was a vast gas-proof shelter. Sewell arrived and reassured Robert that all was well. Robert took him to see *Marie Antoinette* and decided that after all he was quite good in it — perhaps he should have braved the premiere. However, there was now New York to enjoy and Robert tried vainly to encourage Sewell in his sight seeing, but Sewell remained unmoved as Robert expounded on the joys of New York with all the enthusiasm of a vacuum cleaner salesman to an intransigent housewife. Sewell did however learn to love waffles with maple syrup.

Rehearsals for *Wilde* started on September 26th. Norman Marshall had marked the moves out on the stage in chalk. Robert looked at them. He looked at Norman. Then he tiptoed gingerly from one to the next, emphasizing each half step. 'I had no idea,' he told Marshall, 'that *Oscar Wilde* was to be performed on Broadway by midgets.' The chalk marks were removed.

Robert was distressed to read in the papers that the Royal Navy had been mobilized — and he hadn't heard from home. What, he wondered, was the situation there? Days and weeks passed and there was no post from his mother. Then a pile of letters arrived. She had been addressing them to the St Regis Hotel — but they had tracked Robert down and forwarded them to the St Moritz. He wrote back reassuringly, only slightly chiding her — after all, one saint was much like another. 'I wish I didn't believe that the whole thing was a pretty put-up job. I cannot understand what Chamberlain meant by "Peace with Honour". His self-satisfaction is alarming . . . nor can I find any difference between the terms at Munich and Hitler's second demands. However I really can't worry about it but you must admit that the public in England has been hopelessly misled over the real issue.'

Keeping his mind firmly off Europe's troubles and indeed his own impending first night, he launched into learning about New York with a vengeance. The weather was sunny. He haunted the art galleries and the theatres, went to Harlem on Saturday night, and ate hamburgers endlessly.

It was a good season in New York — Katharine Hepburn was in *The Philadelphia Story,* Raymond Massey was being *Abraham Lincoln in Illinois,* Tallulah Bankhead was in Lillian Hellman's *Little Foxes.* Frederick March, Maurice Evans, Laurette Taylor, Judith Anderson, Katharine Cornell and Laurence Olivier were also to be found on the Great White Way.

Gilbert Miller's name was not in anyway connected with *Oscar Wilde* when it opened at the Fulton Theatre in New York. He was rather nervous of the subject matter. There was an enormous morality campaign going on in New York at the time, and moreover a few years before Miller had been prosecuted for putting on a play about lesbians. He had had to promise the court he would never produce a salacious play again. And for all he knew, in the prevailing climate they might just consider *Oscar Wilde* salacious material. There was no censor in New York and although Miller thought it a fine play he wasn't sure that the police wouldn't raid it and close it down. He couldn't take the chance of having his name involved.

Robert wasn't sure he wanted to be involved in it either. Before going to the theatre he consoled himself with a chocolate ice cream soda at Rumplemeyers. He sucked on the straws and wondered if he should make a run for it. Could they sue him? As the straws made that sound that heralds the empty glass, he decided he was more frightened of not going to the theatre than of going. On that night of October 10th the play opened to less than $300 advance booking, but there was no raid. There was, however, a certain amount of hysteria in the audience, and Robert took twenty curtain calls. First night audiences in New York tended to be rather blasé. In fact they were called 'The Deathwatch', but they knew a hit when they saw one — and this was definitely a hit. Robert had never before experienced this reaction. Of course he had had a great success in London, but British audiences even when rapturous remain more subdued. 'Bravos' echoed through the Fulton theatre and by the next day they were being shouted all over the city.

The critics happily agreed with the rest of the audience. Brooks Atkinson of the *New York Times* wrote 'Speaking some of the most perfect apophthegms an actor ever got hold of, Mr Morley knows how to phrase them with grace and humour and how to distinguish a cultivated wit from a common wisecracker. As far as the part goes, one feels instinctively that this is the truth of Oscar Wilde, who was no cheap phenomenon but a 'lord of language' as he once immodestly phrased it. Mr Morley is an actor of very superior stature whose coming into our theatre is an event.' Richard Watts Jr., of the *Herald Tribune* raved: 'The wittiest play in town. A curiously enthralling work, beautifully played by Robert Morley. He is nothing short of brilliant. The most impressive drama of the new season.'

Gilbert Miller lost no time in connecting his name with the play. Moreover he decided after those reviews to put Robert's name up on lights on Broadway. 'Robert Morley in Oscar Wilde,' he told Robert. Ever aware of the *double entendre* Robert preferred 'Robert Morley as Oscar Wilde', and his name lit up Broadway.

In London, Peter Bull was engaged in the gruelling task of production, yet it was a labour of love. His work in *Marie Antoinette* had not made him a film star, but it did provide the capital for Peter Bull Ltd., and he was at last going to produce Robert's play, *Goodness How Sad!* in the West End. This play, set in a theatrical boarding house in the provinces, had delighted Perranporth audiences. All kinds of thespians met under the stern eyes of the landlady, from circus acts to touring players — and thrown into their midst was a real film star escaping his consuming public in these somewhat

67

impossible surroundings. Although the Munich crisis had had a dampening effect on British spirits Peter wasn't to be deterred. Before his departure for New York Robert had persuaded Tyrone Guthrie to direct it. Pauline Letts, who had created the part of the ingenue at Perranporth, wasn't available for the West End, having retired to home, children and domesticity. Roger Furse did the sets again, and Judith Furse and Frith Banbury retained their original roles. Bull himself had originally had a part, but he didn't feel he could cope with both producing and acting, so Arthur Hambling took over his role. Mary Merrall took the part of the landlady. This was a brilliant piece of casting, suggested by Robert. Miss Merrall had up till that time been noted for rather heavy melodrama. In fact years before, Robert and a friend who was sharing digs, Max Adrian, were lounging about the Samovar, a rather theatrical coffee house. Both out of work, they were wondering what to do with themselves. The theatre, perhaps? Max procured a newspaper and began reading aloud through the listings. Robert was throwing out the occasional disparaging remark with all the arrogance of the young and unemployed actor. Max came to the Lyceum. *'The Old Curiosity Shop',* he read. 'With Mary Merrall as Little Nell.' 'Well,' Robert sucked in his breath, 'that will be . . . ' 'What will it be, Mr Morley?' came an imperious voice behind him. It was Mary Merrall. She had rather saved him from himself. Hugh Sinclair, a very popular leading man, was agreeable to playing the romantic lead. Llewellyn Rees, having saved them so much money in California, was hired once again to look after finances.

The newspapers prior to the first night were full of stories about Peter Bull being the youngest producer in the West End, and he persuaded the celebrated Viennese actress Elizabeth Bergner to come to the first night on October 19th, thus ensuring some publicity. Robert wasn't at all convinced about the viability of the play and was amazed at the reviews his mother sent him. W. A. Darlington wrote: 'Robert Morley has the sure touch of an actor dramatist and as he is here writing of a subject he knows thoroughly, his play achieves both humour and sincerity with equal ease.' Another critic, Archie De Bear 'enjoyed every moment of it and found it so much more entertaining than any other play I have seen for quite a while that my own impulse was to exclaim, *Gladness How Good!*' The advance bookings were not good, but neither had they been for *Oscar Wilde* before those spectacular reviews. Though *Goodness How Sad!* was not in the same league it looked like being a moderate success.

That same week *Marie Antoinette* opened at the Empire, Leicester Square. The English reviewers found the film over-long. C. A. Lejeune thought it much too gloomy, but all the critics agreed it was a fitting part for Norma Shearer's return and moreover a block-busting performance by Robert. In fact *The Times* led its review: 'Mr Morley's portrait of Louis XVI. . . is a remarkable and very sympathetic performance, highly realistic but without a trace of caricature, touching but quite without sentimentality, an objective study of clumsy, halting goodness.'

It was rather obvious now that all the English newspapers should write of the triple success and many bemoaned the fact that it was the Americans who had really made Robert a star. Reading the papers, Daisy Morley decided that this was the moment to send Robert his tail coat which he had left behind. He must, after all be meeting the right kind of people now. Robert declined. 'One of my ambitions,' he wrote to her, 'is never to wear tails again.' His mother was disappointed. In her version of society gentlemen wore tails.

Just as there is no more abject a feeling than to be a failure in New York, no success is quite so heady and Robert absolutely loved being the man of the moment. The invitations poured in — to dine, to write, to speak, and Robert could resist none of them. After all, how long could it last? By the end of October he finally believed that Oscar Wilde would be at the Fulton Theatre through the winter. He moved out of his hotel into a flat on East 57th Street which he shared with John Buckmaster who was playing Lord Alfred Douglas. He even had a pianola installed for his amusement. He was tenuously putting down roots in what

69

he called 'the nicest town in the world'.

Robert has always enjoyed watching glamorous people and New York was in its way even better for it than Hollywood, where the acting community kept so much to itself. Robert spent an entire afternoon in the lobby of the St Moritz. Although he was kept busy himself signing autographs, his eyes were peeled for Greta Garbo. He had heard she was coming to stay and he wanted to watch her check in; he also wanted to watch everyone else's reaction to her — that was part of the fun. At the famous nightclub 21 one night a rumour swept through that Joan Crawford was dining. Robert jumped to his feet and gazed around the room. Then he sat down, a stricken look on his face. 'I forgot,' he explained. 'I've already met her.'

Though fascinated by the famous, who, he still maintained, were a different breed of people, he was never impressed to the point of neglecting to express his opinions, and Robert is seldom without strongly-held opinions. At this point it was his views on Chamberlain he was keen to air. Robert Sherwood gave an intimate party one night after the theatre. Small but glittery. The Sherwoods, Helen Hayes, Raymond Massey and Robert — the reigning Broadway stars. 'Chamberlain!' Robert said as the discussion turned to Europe and the fears of war, 'his sort of manoeuvering is too crooked even for a firm of shady solicitors let alone an Empire's foreign policy.' Massey took exception but the others smoothed the argument over. Robert actually enjoyed the argument. He has never been afraid to take the opposite point of view in any given discussion, whether or not he quite believes in it. Lack of information on the subject has also never been a deterrent; if everyone agrees all the time the conversation tends to be rather dull.

Although there had been speculation in Hollywood about Robert's sexual affiliations — mainly because of his brilliant performance both as Oscar Wilde and as the impotent Louis, but also because he was constantly with his secretary-chauffeur, companion and old friend Llewellyn Rees, who was eight years older than Robert and very used to being the butt of jokes about his age — Llewellyn, as one friend put it, even at RADA looked older than God. When Robert heard about the rumours he retorted, 'What? Me a necrophiliac?' — the rumours were totally unfounded. He always had an eye for an attractive woman and in New York that season he found a real beauty: Gene Tierney. She was born in Brooklyn — the best part, and had been educated in Connecticut and Switzerland. That season she had her first part on Broadway, directed by George Abbott, in *Mrs O'Brien Entertains*. Robert would sit in his dressing-room each night, ten red roses from the florist in front of him, trying desperately to compose a line of poetry for each rose — but he never succeeded. As the curtain was about to rise he would tear up all the paper and give the roses to Sewell to deliver to Miss Tierney's dressing-room down the road. Sewell began to get rather bored with this nightly messenger duty but performed it punctiliously. One Sunday he accompanied Robert to Gene's house for lunch at the invitation of her mother. It was his first real meeting with her. All those other evenings he had just delivered the flowers and left. On the way home he told Robert that he had indeed thought she was rather lovely. 'You know,' Robert said, 'I'm not at all sure I'm not in love with the mother.'

While it was standing room only at the Fulton every night, across the Atlantic *Goodness How Sad!* was barely limping along at the Vaudeville. Although the reviews had been good and all the audiences seemed to enjoy it, business hadn't picked up. Peter was convinced that it would, and Robert began sending money to tide the company over what Peter hoped was just a slow start. Surely word of mouth would begin to sell tickets. Robert was sure the main problem was the title, but he hadn't thought of a better one.

The snow arrived for Thanksgiving in 1938. There were gale force winds and the pavements turned to ice. Never being very good at manoeuvering on slippery surfaces, Robert declared that it took hours to get anywhere. Still, he managed two Thanksgiving parties, quite approving of the custom of gorging. In fact he had given a turkey party himself

71

on the eve for the Company but found it rather dull as it was an all-male cast. He was no longer bothered much by autograph hounds as every time he ventured away from the log fire he kept burning in his flat he muffled himself up — coat collar turned up, hat pulled down over his nose. Of course, he sometimes took off the hat. As he handed it to the attendant at the Stork Room one night the girl immediately recognized him. 'Oh, Mr Wilde,' she said, 'Can I please have your autograph?' Robert sighed and wrote: 'Oscar Morley'.

By the first week in December the snow had cleared in a mini-thaw and although business had fallen off a bit in *Oscar Wilde* (they were no longer standing but it was still full house every night), Robert was cheered by the brilliant sunshine. Sewell and Robert were invited to spend the day at Sing-Sing by a policeman friend they had made. It was really Sewell's idea — he had always had a fascination for courts, police and prisons — and Robert was most reluctant. If the sun hadn't been shining he wouldn't have gone at all — it seemed a gloomy prospect. For seven hours they trudged around the prison, smiling and nodding and trying to be inconspicuous, until, exhausted, Robert fell asleep in the electric chair.

Robert's mother was still trying to convince him that there was a lot to be said for Chamberlain, but he remained unmoved. And in New York John Buckmaster's mother, Gladys Cooper, couldn't be less concerned with politics or politicians. She was preparing for a first night. Gladys Cooper had been one of those real untouchable glittering stars for as long as Robert could remember — the kind he would have waited for all day in the lobby of an hotel, hoping for a glimpse. She had been a postcard pin-up in the First World War — a Gaiety girl and a West End starring actress. Her leading men had been Owen Nares, Ivor Novello and Gerald du Maurier. Robert would never forget her in *The Last Mrs Cheyney,* nor would he forget the memory of the moment she stood on the staircase in *Cynara.* She was not only beautiful but elegant. He was highly excited by the notion of being able to give a party in her honour at the apartment he shared with her son.

72

Being a star in New York meant not only glamorous parties, tea with Mrs Vanderbilt, and seeing and being seen at night clubs. Robert was also interviewed almost endlessly, invited to write for the *New York Times,* and to speak at functions ranging from a lecture on the theatre at a girls' school (where he managed to speak for the first time in public for twenty minutes without notes and was very pleased with himself) to a charity performance at Madison Square Garden (where 'I just went out and said I was pleased to be there in aid of a great cause which I discovered was something to do with getting the Jews out of Germany. There were thirty thousand people there and I was about the only Christian. They made over seventy thousand dollar').

Richard Collett, a Director of the Savoy Group of hotels, and Henry Sherek, a London producer in charge of shows at the Dorchester, Ritz, Mayfair and Carlton, came to New York. They were looking for American cabaret artists for their hotels. But Sherek, also interested in theatrical productions, found himself on Broadway. There in enormous lights he saw 'Robert Morley'. 'Who is he?' he asked his colleague. He thought he knew all the stars, having been involved in the business all his life. 'I know Morley quite well,' Collett told him. 'He's an English actor.' And knowing Robert's delight in an evening out, he asked him to the various night club entertainments they had come to see.

So, after the evening performance, Robert set off with them to supper and the floor show. At each restaurant, when they entered, conversation stopped and hisses of recognition filled the air. 'That's Robert Morley,' the diners whispered. Sherek was very impressed. Why had Robert had to come to New York to make such a success? He went to see *Oscar Wilde* — and was as impressed by his performance as he had been by his fame. Just before sailing for home he went to see Robert. 'If you ever want to do a costume play in England,' he told him, 'just let me know.'

By Christmas Robert found that his enchantment with America hadn't worn off and he was considering taking out papers to stay, though he hadn't got around to it. Hollywood had offered him *The Hunchback of Notre Dame*. He asked Sewell about it, taking it that Sewell was better read than himself. 'Terrible part,' his friend told him. 'He never says anything.' So Robert turned it down, and Charles Laughton got his own back. Robert was getting masses of plays sent to him all the time now but hadn't found anything he really wanted to do next. He was rather keen on the idea of taking the Perranporth players around the world but wondered if he and Peter would ever raise enough money. His immediate goal was to run *Oscar Wilde* right through the season, as few plays on Broadway lasted that long.

Christmas day was sunny but the wind was biting. Robert stayed in bed past two in the afternoon as he had been to rather a good Christmas Eve party. He was invited by Mrs Vanderbilt to a party that night, but had also been invited to one at Gladys Cooper's apartment. He decided without hesitation to go to Gladys.

When Robert wasn't on stage, at a party, or being his own press agent, he was writing plays. Sunday afternoons would be reading days, usually in the apartment he shared with John Buckmaster. Gladys would take a part, A. E. Matthews another, but mostly the reading would be Robert's. (He loves reading aloud — especially his own work.) The plays, however, seldom proceeded beyond the first act. New York was too distracting to allow for prolonged creativity. He had a brilliant idea which he worked on periodically. It was to be called *Younger Than Ever* — a woman starts out at about seventy in the first act and gets younger as the play progresses. But he abandoned it, having not only decided that it would be impossible to cast, but also that he hadn't any idea of how he could possibly end it.

In 1939, Robert was indeed nominated for an Academy Award as all the critics had predicted. It hadn't been a good year for Hollywood. There had been lots of expensive pictures made, *Marie Antoinette* being just one of them, and there had been a forty per cent drop at the box office. The award banquet, the eleventh, was held on February 23rd at the Biltmore Hotel. The best picture award went to Frank

Capra's *You Can't Take It With You; Marie Antoinette* wasn't even nominated in that category. Bette Davis beat Norma Shearer for her performance in *Jezebel*, and Spencer Tracy was hailed as best actor for *Boys Town*. Robert lost out as best supporting actor to Walter Brennan. Still, he couldn't be too unhappy. As is frequently said, the public remembers the nominations and seldom the actual awards, and to be nominated for his very first film appearance was praise indeed. Most of the publicity that year went to George Bernard Shaw. When the eighty-two year-old playwright was told that he had won an oscar for *Pygmalion* he was furious: 'My position as a playwright is known throughout the world. To offer me an award of this sort is an insult, as if they had never heard of me — and it's very likely they never had. Of course it's a good film. It's the only film.'

In March, Sewell, who had come the previous September for two weeks, left to return to England on the *Mauritania*. Robert was going to play through the season and then there was talk of a tour in the States. *Goodness How Sad!* was still limping along at the Vaudeville — kept alive by consistent if small audiences, the occasional fifty pounds Robert would send over, and blessings from heaven such as the sale of the film rights. It kept going through April but closed on May 6th. Robert had never seen it in the West End — but he did send a cheque for the management and cast to have an outing on the night after they closed. A good time was had by all with dinner at Rules and a visit to the theatre, thus taking the sting out of the closure.

Oscar Wilde closed at the end of May and Robert decided the moment had come to write to Mayer in Hollywood — after all, hadn't he said to contact him when he was out of work? Robert's agent counselled against it. 'Let them come to you,' he told Robert. 'Nonsense,' Robert said, 'he told me to let him know when I was interested in making another picture.' So he wrote. A letter from an underling at the studios came back informing Robert that when Mr Mayer had need of his services he would be approached through the correct channels. So much for Hollywood.

75

CHAPTER SIX

GILBERT MILLER HAD BEEN VERY KEEN to keep Robert in
America to do a national tour of *Oscar Wilde*. But summer
was coming and July was the time to be back in Perranporth.
It still wasn't Robert's idea of a proper Cornish village but
this time the house approached it. It was called the Villa Bel
Fiori, was several stories high and had a lovely garden. By
now the troupe was well established and there was no
trouble selling seats. It was possible to use the splendid
'house full' signs every night. But it was a hot summer and
the small building got rather unbearable as it was impossible
to open the windows with the traffic roaring past on the main
road outside. Llewellyn Rees came to join the company that
year. He directed the first offering — Robert and Peter's
favourite, *Springtime for Henry*. 'Well,' he said, 'I sort of tried
to move people around Robert. I never actually directed
him.' Pamela Brown had joined the company that year and
she was in it, too. Sewell was a frequent visitor. The whole
company fitted into the house and they were looked after by
a middle-aged local lady who came daily. Every morning she
would wheel an enormous pram up the garden path, a baby
barely visible in the depths of it. In the evening the baby sat
up high — the bottom of the pram being filled with purloined
provisions, the company suspected. But no one really
minded. The theatre was a success, and besides everyone
was trying to be very jolly. Europe was in gloom. War was

imminent. Everyone in the Perranporth company tried very hard to convince themselves and everyone else that there would be no war. Everyone, that is, except Jack Minster, the one member of the company who was not only certain that there would be a war but also that England would lose.

The Perranporth Players had acquired star quality. Whereas the first season they had been a group of out-of-work actors, tolerated by the locals, now they were stars. Regular forays were made from London by other stars, and the local post office buzzed with transatlantic cables. One day there was a parcel from New York for Robert. It contained the first act of a new comedy by George Kaufman called *The Man Who Came To Dinner,* based on the character of his friend Alexander Woolcott, an acerbic New York broadcaster, writer and wit, and member of the famous Algonquin round table. Woolcott's first choice to play Sheridan Whiteside was John Barrymore, but he wrote in a letter, 'we all knew that even then his mind was so far gone that he could never have remembered the lines. Curiously enough, my nomination for the part was Robert Morley.' Woolcott, like everyone else in New York, had seen *Oscar Wilde* and thought that Robert had handled a difficult characterization with tact, wit and charm. He rather liked the idea of having this caricature of himself handled with the same qualities. Robert half read it and handed it over to Sewell, who read it and gave it to Llewellyn. In deck chairs under the sun in Cornwall they both pronounced it decidedly common — certainly not to be considered. Robert sent it back with regrets, and not by air.

Robert chose the last production that season — *Doctor Knock,* a translation from the French. Robert was well pleased with his part but the other members of the company weren't, so Robert tended to stay out of the way of minor grumblings. One day he decided to drive down to Land's End with Sewell. He had forgotten that weeks before he had invited some people to tea that day. John Buckmaster had told him to be sure to look up his sister and father when he got back to England. Robert hadn't, but John had written the same message to his father, Captain Herbert Buckmaster who founded and ran Buck's Club in London, an establishment originally intended for comrades in the Boer War. The Club was closed for its annual holiday in August, and he had taken a house in Veryan which he shared with Grace, soon to be his third wife, and Joan, his daughter by his first marriage to Gladys Cooper. So Buck, ever conscious of the social graces, had written to Robert weeks before and arranged a meeting.

The three of them arrived and were fairly horrified by the crowds and the traffic in Perranporth, having expected, like Robert on his first arrival there, a pretty, sedate Cornish village. Furthermore, the Women's Institute was firmly closed for the day until the evening performance, and there was no one at home at the villa. Wandering on the beach Joan spotted Pamela Brown who told her that Robert had gone out sightseeing. Buck was not pleased. But they went that night to see *Doctor Knock* and backstage afterwards Robert apologised profusely. He thought Joan was the most attractive young lady he had seen and was genuinely sorry to have missed an afternoon with her. Buck still wasn't pleased; an invitation to tea is not the kind of thing anyone with proper manners forgets. Grace and Joan were slightly cheered when Robert assured them most forcefully that there would be no war.

Three days later war was declared and the air of tension that had been hanging over the summer became one of complete gloom. The theatre closed immediately. Several members of the company enlisted straight away but others— Peter, Robert and Llewellyn among them—sat around at the villa wondering what to do next. Jack Minster declared that they would be overrun with Germans within weeks, if not days. They studied pamphlets from the Ministry wondering what use they could be in the country at war. Robert at first decided that the fire service was the only possible place for him but then, realizing that it would involve ladders and heights, rejected the idea. He began to hold classes for conscientious objectors, pretending to be an examining magistrate. His considered opinion was that the lot of them would have a difficult time keeping out of the army. It wasn't that he was particularly afraid of being shot — that seemed as likely to happen to a civilian as to a soldier. Battles were the least of his worries; it was the authoritarian aspect of the services that worried him — it was like going back to school.

The trains back to London were impossible. People stood crowded in the corridors, their holidays cut short as England got about the business of being at war. Jack Minster, in spite of his forebodings about the future, married Barbara Cochran, another member of the company, in Perranporth. Their honeymoon drive would eventually take them back to London. Robert was in no hurry and he decided that going with them was the best way of getting back, and much to their amazement he joined them on their honeymoon. On the way he decided to take them on a detour to see his Aunt Betty, his mother's eldest sister. He primed Jack to be very careful about what he said. Like Daisy, Betty was a keen Chamberlain supporter. Jack nervously kept his silence but Robert couldn't help himself. Something about his Empire-minded family always brought out the worst in him and he had a terrible row with his aunt.

The war in London hadn't really got started. Robert took a flat in Whitehall Court where Llewellyn moved in as his secretary again. Gilbert Miller was very busy organizing the American tour of *Oscar Wilde,* and Robert was looking forward to going back to America. He met Nick Phipps one day in the West End and they were reminiscing on the street corner about Perranporth. Nick rather chided him on standing up the Buckmasters that day. Robert admitted it had been a mistake as when they did meet he had been completely enchanted by Joan, but as she was a soldier's daughter he thought she had probably enlisted as soon as war was declared. Robert also thought she would not be impressed by his own determination to stay out of the war as long as possible. Nick was an old friend. As Buck had gone off to Birmingham in readiness for local government in case of invasion and Joan, whose flatmates were actresses and away on tours, was alone in the flat, she moved into Buck's Club to keep an eye on it for him. In those days women were not to be seen in the Club and she had to stay firmly in her room out of sight. That was rather tedious so she spent a good deal of time out, visiting and dining, and quite often it was with Nick. 'I'm having dinner with her tonight,' he told Robert. 'Why don't you come along?'

When Joan arrived at the restaurant that night she found Robert waiting for her and a message from Nick that he was very sorry but he couldn't make it. That evening began a courtship that their friends still speak of with amazement. Joan, a very attractive young lady, was not without suitors. She was quiet and elegant. And this whirlwind of an actor didn't seem at all suited to her. Instead of roses this time he plied her with gifts of roller skates and a doll of Chamberlain which when wound up played 'God Save The King'. The roses were being received by a rather amazed Ambrosine Phillpotts.

Ambrosine was involved in a tour of Robert's play, *Goodness How Sad!* Peter had sold his rights to a man called Barry Jackson. The air raids hadn't started yet but the theatrical world was very nervous and planning only in the very short term. The Coliseum offered Barry Jackson a three-week engagement with the play. Ambrosine was to play the part created by Judith Furse; Mary Merrall was still in it, and the *ingénue* was Sarah Churchill. The huge theatre was the last place for this charming but small play. Yet it worked, the company was happy together, and thought it might be possible to carry on. Ambrosine had been a big success at Hull and so she rang up the theatre there and the show was booked immediately. She had the same success with the Hammersmith Theatre. So the tour began. Ambrosine had never met Robert. She did, however, know Joan. Gladys Cooper had married Philip Merivale, the Canadian actor, who had three children. One of them, Rosamund, now Joan's stepsister and flatmate, had worked at Hull with Ambrosine and they had become firm friends, so Ambrosine was a frequent visitor to the flat. But, Ambrosine, very involved in the play, didn't know that Joan and Robert had even met. Red roses began to arrive nightly in Hull, then Hammersmith, from Robert with the message — 'Keep up the good work.' Ambrosine thought Robert was pleased that she had found dates for the show and that the roses were a token of his gratitude. At least that is what she thought until she heard from Buck. He rang her and said she must discourage Joan from marrying Robert. Acting wasn't the kind of solid profession he expected his son-in-law to follow. It was an insecure business and he had no doubts that Robert would fail to make a living. Buck preferred someone more handsome and established — an officer and a gentleman. Surely, he begged Ambrosine, she could break up this friendship? He had mentioned to Robert that Ambrosine was one of Joan's great friends. Then Ambrosine understood the flowers. Robert wanted her on his side. She told Buck that she planned to stay well out of it. And she did.

Gabriel Pascal, a film director described alternately as a madman and a genius, decided he wanted Robert in a film. He wanted Robert to star as Undershaft, the munitions millionaire in *Major Barbara*. Robert was full of regrets — any other time he would be more than delighted but he was committed to going to America on tour. He had waged a successful and whirlwind courtship, which surprised all their friends. Joan had been brought up with the theatre — many of her friends as well as her family were involved in it — but she had also been to Heathfield, an exclusive girls' school, and to finishing school in France. Joan had friends in all branches of the arts as well as society, and they thought this quiet, elegant young woman would be more attracted by the kind of suitor Buck preferred. But Robert made her laugh. He was scheduled to go to the States and Joan decided to go with him. They planned to be married in America. After all her mother was there and her brother, John. Gilbert Miller was more than delighted to be able to help. He had known Joan since she was a child. She would travel as part of the company. Never mind that it was an all-male cast — these problems could be overcome. However, Pascal was not a man to take no for an answer. He wanted Robert for his film. He contacted friends at the Home Office, convinced that his film would win the war. Was the image of Oscar Wilde one that the British government really wanted to project abroad in these difficult times? Certainly the effete poet was not symbolic of Britain in the 1940s. Might not the Americans get the wrong idea? Travel was very restricted in this period. It all had to be cleared with the Home Office. Joan's passport came back cancelled. So did Robert's. There would be no tour that season, and Robert agreed to film *Major Barbara*.

They decided to get married in England. Llewellyn's brother was a canon at St Paul's. Llewellyn was dispatched to arrange it all. He came back and rather shyly told them that the Dean had said, 'No,' going on to explain that as neither of them were churchgoers he saw no obligation to carry out the function. So they opted for a civil ceremony. Rumours of the romance were stirring about London but Joan had a dread of publicity. Her childhood had been rather too full of it with her glamorous, energetic mother. From babyhood through to near adolescence she had had to pose for the famous postcards and she often had to share her mother rather too much with the public. The wedding was to be kept secret. Joan was back in her flat in de Vere Gardens. Ros Merivale had returned from her tour and so had Dorothy Hyson, the other member of the flat. Llewellyn was to make all the arrangements, quietly. But rumours spread fast and he found himself in Robert's flat in Whitehall Court telling all who rang that Robert was abroad and he had heard of no wedding plans. *Major Barbara* was in production and Robert was safe at Denham Studios. The night before the wedding there was the inevitable stag party, though a rather subdued one by some standards. Peter Bull, Sewell Stokes, Llewellyn and Robert went off to Islington where at the ABC Robert ate at least eight fishcakes (a life-long particular favourite) and then onto Collins' Music Hall where they had a box. The master of ceremonies had begun his speech: 'Tonight, ladies and gentlemen, we have in the audience –' and Robert began to sink lower and lower in his seat, dreading the moment when he would have to stand and take a bow — but the comedian introduced a boxer they had never heard of and the spotlight didn't fall on Robert that night. Danger passed, he was rather annoyed.

The wedding was scheduled for the next day, February 23rd, 1940, at Caxton Hall. Robert's mother was invited and his sister Margaret. Joan's flatmates were there and so was her father, having become reconciled to the wedding. But that was all — no one else was invited. The preliminary arrangements had been completed by Llewellyn but there were still forms to fill in before the service. Leaving the few guests in the ante-room, Robert and Joan found themselves faced with a very long-winded registrar. He had previously worked in an office next to the building owned by Gladys' second husband, Neville Pearson. The registrar went into lengthy detail about occasions on which he had caught a glimpse of the famous lady coming to visit her husband. Finally he got down to the business at hand: 'The bride's father,' he asked looking down at his form. 'Is he still alive?' Robert sighed heavily. 'I'll just go and look,' he said.

There was no reception after the ceremony. They only had the weekend for their honeymoon as Robert had to be back at Denham on Monday for the film. They drove down to Tewkesbury where there was a very nice hotel, and where one of Robert's uncles lived if they felt like visiting. On the way the car got a flat tyre. Neither of them had any idea of how to change a wheel and so they stood by the side of the road until rescued by a passing motorist.

The next morning they sent for the newspapers. Joan, it was true, avoided publicity at all costs — but still it was nice to see what people said about you. All the English papers reported that Gladys Cooper's daughter had married an actor. It was true that one of them called Robert 'internationally famous as an actor' but he wasn't very pleased with second billing. Joan's brother John cabled from New York: 'I just told you to look her up. Aren't you overdoing it?' They did manage to visit Robert's uncle who was horrified that Robert was not in uniform and had rather pointedly, considering his age and infirmity, dressed as a scoutmaster for the meeting.

The newlyweds got a nine months' lease on a flat in Arlington House next to the Ritz Hotel. The price was ludicrously low because no one wanted to live in central London and off Piccadilly was about as central as you could get. They expected the bombing to start at any moment. Robert went down to Denham daily to film and Joan got a pekinese called Mitzi. Visitors came frequently to the flat. Ambrosine brought her peke and played bridge with Robert. It was a beautifully furnished flat, but Robert's mother, still looking on the gloomy side, commented that it was 'nice' some people could afford to have a white sofa in these troubled times.

There were, however, difficulties at Denham. Pascal was a genius with a quick temper. He was an inspired director but could never be accused of being methodical. Money meant nothing to him . . . his or anyone else's. Artistic integrity was his guiding light. If a scene wasn't right, no matter how much time and money had been spent, it was scrapped and started again. The actor engaged to play Cusins wasn't working out and he was dismissed. Rex Harrison took over the part but it meant time was needed for re-thinking. Which scenes would need to be reshot? 'Rex Harrison,' Pascal told Robert, 'has the face of a tortured Christ.' 'Tortured by too tight shoes,' murmured David Lean, the editor. Robert was furious he hadn't said it himself. Filming was halted for a month. Everyone would have to be paid during the month, of course; they couldn't be expected to find work to fill in that period. Pascal was delighted that Robert did manage to. Sewell had written a film version of the life of Leslie Stuart, the Manchester-born composer who had written 'Soldiers Of The Queen' and 'Lily Of Laguna'. It was called *You Will Remember*. Robert spent his lay-off from *Major Barbara* being the composer. He was two weeks late getting back to the Shaw film but that didn't worry Pascal. They were on location now for the summer in Devon. Shooting was to be at Dartington Hall, and Robert and Joan found a small cottage nearby. The British forces were evacuated from Dunkirk, small boats arrived on the coast, but that summer in Devon was relatively peaceful — as peaceful as any place could be with German planes crossing the Channel and Gabriel Pascal directing.

When they returned to London, the blitz had started. Bombs fell nearby and the flat reverberated, each strike seeming to come closer. Robert generally dived for cover but Joan, ever a fatalist, merely readjusted the lamps which had been dislodged by the blast. A good deal of time had to be spent in the basement, sheltering, which after a while Joan flatly refused to do. Hired cars would no longer come to Piccadilly to take Robert to the studios. He usually had to leave at five in the morning to be finished with make-up in time for shooting, as each hair in the beard he wore for the part had to be placed on his chin separately. Joan had to drive him. The heavy raids on September 15th decided it. They left Arlington House and went to stay with Buck and Grace in Wentworth where they had rented a house, and Robert commuted daily to the studios from there. The lease was soon to run out, though Robert wasn't quite sure that was why Grace and Buck gave up the house. He rather suspected that they were bored with having him to stay.

Robert found a cottage to rent near Slough. It looked as though the film might go on forever and this was very convenient for the studios, and also the rent was reasonable. All the preparations for the move were in hand when the sisters who owned the property suddenly demanded twice the rent. Robert considered this pure blackmail and declined to rent their house. He had seen a freehold cottage advertised for sale in *The Times* that morning. It was in the Thames-side village of Wargrave, or rather high on a hill on the outskirts of the village. It was fairly square, very small and rather unattractive and surrounded by what looked like swamp land but it was cheap and Robert saw potential — also he was in a hurry. It would, however, be some weeks before it

85

was even habitable, so he and Joan went to a hotel — a splendid old Tudoresque structure in Egham called Great Fosters. John Gielgud was staying there, as was Marie Tempest. They were all making different films at Denham.

Since *Short Story,* Marie Tempest had been very fond of Robert but he had neglected to visit her on his return from America and she wasn't speaking to him. In the dining room, each guest was assigned his own table; Robert and Joan had one — next to them was John Gielgud's and beyond him Marie Tempest's. John was in the middle in every sense of the word, conveying the conversation from one table to the next. But the silence was finally broken. Robert was in bed with a quinsy throat. He suffered from them regularly before the invention of penicillin. Joan, walking the peke in the huge garden, told Marie about it. 'Don't worry about it, dear,' the grand lady told her. 'I had double quinsy, going up the Yangtze.' Because of the quinsy, which was very infectious, they thought, Joan and Robert had moved their beds apart in the vast bedroom. One night a bomb fell, the windows shattered, and Joan and Robert simultaneously sprang from bed and met in the middle of the room, where they found themselves clutching each other under a huge crystal chandelier which vibrated ominously. Luckily it remained fixed. The glass from the window had been adequately contained behind the heavy velvet curtains. As they were returning to bed there was a knock on the door. It was the porter to inform them that all was well: 'The bomb fell on the servants' quarters.'

Major Barbara was nearly eleven months in production. Part of the delay was caused by the necessity for the cast and crew to retire to air raid shelters everytime there was an alert. The shelter was small, crowded and airless, and no one was very pleased to be there, least of all Wendy Hiller who was starring in the title role. One day she looked around and noticed that the director was not there in the shelter with them. Come to think of it, she had never seen him there. Pascal was not the kind of man to bother about safety and was usually setting up the next shot. Robert, ever eager to have a bit of fun, told her that there was a special executive shelter under the great lake at Denham and that, of course, was where Pascal spent the alerts with the other VIPs. Alert over, Wendy furiously demanded to be included in the executive shelter next time. Pascal, clueless, wondered what in heaven's name she was talking about. Robert giggled quietly in a corner as he watched.

George Bernard Shaw came to visit the filming from time to time. Robert was pleased to meet the man whose words had originally decided him to be an actor and declared him the only 'saint' he ever met. Shaw liked to keep an eye on Pascal. *Major Barbara* went on and on, and finally he intervened, writing to Pascal:

'My dear Gabriel,

As I feared you have made a worse financial mess of Barbara than you did of Pygmalion. Things have now come to a crisis at which the film has already cost twice what it should. Yet it is still unfinished. The financiers won't go on; the cast is exhausted and sulky; and you have lost your head . . .

Now here are my instructions which you must obey like a lamb. You will finish screening the script without a single retake, until you have it complete. When it is finished, and not until then, you will go through the rushes and be satisfied with what is good enough, no matter how much better you could make it if you had another hundred thousand pounds and another six months. You must finish, finish, finish at all sacrifice until a Barbara film is ready for release no matter how far it may fall short of the film of which you dream.'

But it was July when Shaw wrote that. In December the film was finally finished shooting. And the Wargrave cottage was ready. Joan and Robert moved into their home — Fairmans. Joan's nanny came with them to keep house.

Although he hated it, Robert was by this time resigned to the war and thought perhaps the Royal Air Force was the place for him. Filming over, he was called to Reading to report for his physical. But he did not pass it with flying colours. He was classified pretty far down the list, but the man behind the desk would give him no clue to the medical reasons. Robert began to suspect he wasn't in good health. 'Is it my heart?' he asked worriedly, but the man would tell him nothing. 'I shall read to you,' he told Robert, 'a list of occupations for which you are eligible. State your preference.'

Robert said he'd like to be a cook.

'Why?'

'When the war is over I shall have a trade,' Robert told him. 'I may need one.'

The official decided that he was being sent up. 'I think,' he told Robert, who was growing more and more annoyed by this authoritarian manner, 'a man of your education should pull his weight. Try again.'

'I should like,' Robert said finally, 'to sit in a little room in Reading and tell everyone else what to do.'

'I'm putting you down as a clerk, special duties,' the man said through now firmly clenched teeth.

'What sort of duties?'

'You stay in the control room until it is blown to pieces. Good day.'

But luckily the man in Reading didn't get his wish. Neither did Robert get his to take his place. Somewhere in the Ministry of War it was decided that the best place for Robert for the duration was to remain acting. As long as he was in work there was no chance of being called up. Llewellyn Rees was now Secretary of Equity, the Actors' Union, and every month he had the pleasure of deferring Robert. Actresses were allowed to be out of work for two weeks before being called up but men had to be constantly employed. They could also be called upon to do six weeks' work for ENSA.

But he had to find a play to do. Robert remembered Sherek's offer made in New York. 'If you ever want to do a costume play in England — just let me know.' Norman

Ginsbury had written *Viceroy Sarah, Week in the Sun,* and new versions of a couple of Ibsen plays. His latest work was about the Prince Regent, George IV, and was called *The First Gentleman.* Various producers had taken options on it but it was still unproduced. It seemed ideal for Charles Laughton — and rather used to the comparison by now, Robert thought it would be right for him. Well, right enough in the circumstances: he had to be on the stage, doing what he was best at, or he would find himself in uniform behind a desk doing no one any good.

Robert brought the play — rather dogeared — to Henry Sherek, who was staying at the Ritz. But Sherek wasn't in the play-producing business at the moment; he was about to rejoin the Army for the duration. 'After the war,' he told Robert, who wasn't pleased. He needed a play now.

Then Robert found one by Edward Percy that he decided would be right for him, and there would be a long tour. It was about a fence who has an antique shop for a cover. He is blackmailed and eventually kills his blackmailer with a poison dart. Robert didn't care for the title and decided to call it *Play With Fire.* Jack Minster was in it and Ambrosine Phillpotts, and Henry Cass, who also directed. John Carroll played the blackmailer, the villain of the piece. From the very beginning, at rehearsals in Brighton, the play wasn't going properly. Jack Minster predicted disaster, but then he was always gloomy. Ambrosine didn't think it would work, either — besides, she wasn't feeling very well. Robert began rewriting the play and developed a cold. (Whenever Robert is unhappy about a project he always feels a cold coming on.) He took a suite at the Bedford Hotel in Brighton — two bedrooms, bathroom and sitting-room, then decided that it was a bit extravagant and let Jack have one of the bedrooms.

They opened in February in Brighton and business wasn't very good, to put it mildly. They blamed the war — at least Robert did — the others weren't so sure it wasn't the play, and moved on to Bournemouth. Joan was having teething troubles with the house at Wargrave. There were mice. Robert advised getting a cat. He had plenty of troubles of his own. Jack and Ambrosine were both pressing him to call it quits but he was determined to carry on with the tour. Bournemouth was packed and very lively; the weather was perfect but the play wasn't; moreover Robert didn't feel that the war was going very well. 'I don't mind having my back to the wall, only I can't find one still standing,' he was heard to say, and was reported for careless talk. Stanley Bennett, the electrician at Wargrave, was his local special warden and was deputed to deliver a warning. If it happened again he would be called up.

The play was no better by the time they got to Bath, and nor were the audiences. In Hull they found not only empty houses but also German bombs. They stayed in their dressing-rooms at the theatre listening to the blasts all around and when they let up scurried back to the Beverly Arms Hotel where they were staying. But understandably no one could settle down to sleep. Robert and Ambrosine spent the night playing bezique, which she nearly always won, much to Robert's annoyance. Joan, at Fairmans, trying among all the wartime restrictions to install a bath, heard about the raids and cabled frantically. There was no hope of a phone in Wargrave.

There were three matinees a week in Hull, but still no one came. Robert had put some money into the management to keep the tour going, and even he was beginning to think they ought to call it off, but Edward Percy was keen to keep his play on and so they continued on to Nottingham which was distinctly quieter. Robert had all but given up rewriting and spent the mornings in bed reading detective stories and a good deal of time comparing 'country estates' with Jack. The Minsters had bought a cottage in Buckinghamshire and Barbara kept writing about how successful the garden was. Robert begged Joan for news of their swamp with which to counter.

When they travelled to Liverpool on a Sunday afternoon, Robert thought they had better stay outside in Southport but obviously so did everyone else in the vicinity as Southport was jammed and all the hotels full, so they booked into the Adelphi Hotel in the centre. Ambrosine had been very successful at Liverpool. She had been a local star when she left and this was her first trip back. She was ashamed of being in such a flop and didn't care much for her part. The set was an antique shop and it was crammed with all kinds of paraphernalia, from armour to a sedan chair. Ambrosine felt she spent most of her time on stage standing around being talked at by Robert so, bored to frustration one night, she decided when his back was turned to go and sit in the sedan chair. Robert turned round and found himself talking to air. He began hunting about the junk for her. Ambrosine dissolved into giggles and Henry Cass later scolded them both for being amateurish. Still, there was hardly any audience to see them. Robert was just looking forward to going home for Easter. Liverpool was grim, he could seldom get cigarettes and when he could, he couldn't get any matches. Robert's father had died and he was endlessly trying to sort out his rather complicated affairs. Besides he was involved in a dispute with Pascal about his billing in *Major Barbara*. His name wasn't to appear over the title as Pascal had promised. He thought about suing him, but it wouldn't make any difference — Pascal never changed his mind, and he didn't have any money for damages. 'I shall now resign myself to being a feature player,' he wrote to Joan, 'which is less worrying and may well prove equally remunerative.'

Ambrosine kept beating him at bezique, there were still mice at Fairmans and it was April 1st and freezing cold. Business was worse than ever, if that was possible; however a good dinner at the Crocodile, the best local restaurant, cheered him up a bit, he got a cheque for £60, being Royalties from amateur productions of *Short Story,* and a film offer. But the best news was that the forsythia at Fairmans was flourishing, and that impressed Jack. Business picked up a bit at the end of the Liverpool run, but Robert woke up one Sunday to find the newspapers full of news of the bombing at Belgrade and reviews of *Major Barbara*. Dilys Powell said he was 'a fine actor miscast'; *The Times* that

91

'Robert Morley's performance remains an admirable one in a mistaken key.' But Ernest Betts in the *Sunday Express* said 'he is impressive as Undershaft — his beard alone talks to you.' Generally the critics were baffled by *Major Barbara* and slightly disappointed after the enormous success of *Pygmalion*. It was thought nearly a masterpiece but not quite. With *You Will Remember* (the film about Leslie Stuart which Robert made during the lay-off from *Major Barbara*), the critics didn't expect so much and were pleasantly surprised.

The company packed up in Liverpool and headed for the Opera House in Manchester, a huge and extremely prestigious theatre. Cochran had held the first nights of his spectacular reviews there, and they could be more social and glittery than London openings. It was a difficult theatre to play but it was always packed to the rafters — except this time. On Saturday night *Play With Fire* was anything but packed, and they took in £34. Robert gave up fiddling with the play. It was nearly over now and he had a distinct end-of-term feeling. He went to see Marlene Dietrich in *Seven Sinners,* which he enjoyed, and read Hemingway's new book *For Whom The Bell Tolls,* which he didn't. There were air raid shelters in the hotel and the bomb damage was horrific. The centre of town, the Free Trade Hall and the Princess Theatre were completely burned out. But Robert still found wonderful shops, fifty cigarettes at the station and an almost pre-war dinner at the hotel.

Joan had suspicions that she was pregnant. She wrote to tell him about it. Robert wasn't quite sure how he felt about a baby, he hadn't really thought about it. But he was absolutely sure how he felt about Joan. 'Getting your letters and writing mine are the two things I look forward to all day . . . and I feel that even if I have to go into the RAF nothing will spoil that. I have never enjoyed writing letters before, but then I still don't to anyone else.'

The *Manchester Guardian* gave the play a good notice but it didn't help the business. Robert was elected to the Council of Equity, which meant trips to London after the play. There were alerts in Manchester too, and one night a good deal of gun fire and planes overhead, but they had dropped their bombs on Liverpool. Then Joan wrote that she was sure. They were going to have a baby. Robert's immediate reaction was practical — how he would rearrange the small house: 'We can turn Nan's room into the nursery for the time being. Nan can have my room and we'll get a divan for the dining-room and I can sleep there and we'll eat in the sitting-room. Then after a time we could make your room a nursery. Unless of course they would let us build on.' But that was very unlikely while the war lasted.

At last the tour was over. Robert caught a train back to Wargrave. It had been a disaster and he had lost nearly £500. He was only too glad to give up his rights in *Play With Fire*. Six months later, Percy put his original title back, *Shop At Sly Corner*. John Carroll continued as the villain of the piece and it opened at the St Martins in London and ran about two years.

CHAPTER SEVEN

ROBERT MADE THREE QUICK FILMS. The first, for Warners, was directed by John Harlow. It was a pure propaganda film called *This Was Paris,* and Robert played Van Der Stuyl, a Dutchman who was used as a blind for fifth column work. The next one was made by the Ministry of Economic Warfare. It was made at Ealing Studios and was about the blockade of Germany and called, not surprisingly, *The Big Blockade.* This was directed by Charles Frend. Frank Owen was the commentator and Will Hay had his first straight part. Robert played a German, and *The Times* said it was 'a brave attempt to combine entertainment and instruction'. *The Foreman Went To France* was also made at Ealing and also directed by Charles Frend. This time Robert played a French fifth columnist.

The Man Who Came To Dinner landed on Robert's desk again. Although he had turned it down originally when the authors wanted him to do it in New York, this was an English production and it was wartime. Firth Shephard wanted Robert to play Sheridan Whiteside, the part Monty Wooly had created on Broadway after Robert's refusal. This time Robert said yes — after all, it had been running for two years on Broadway and that was a pretty good recommendation. It would mean being able to stay at Fairmans because they would be playing at the Savoy. It was an enormous show for a 'straight' play — thirty-six speaking parts. Sheridan Whiteside was a thinly-disguised Alexander

Woolcott, who had recently been in London reporting home on the blitz and was known to the British public, though not as well as in America. Whiteside arrives to do a broadcast from an average home in the mid-west and breaks his leg. Then the acid, irascible writer and critic and celebrity has to stay. He plays havoc with the household, bizarre characters come and go, and he demands constant attention, making everyone's life a misery. Other parts were caricatures of Noël Coward, the Marx brothers and other well-known personalities. It was a fast moving, wise-cracking farce. The long-suffering secretary who tries hard to keep the situation under control was to be played by Coral Browne who had shared Robert's success in *The Great Romancer.*

The play was to have a brief out-of-town warm-up in Birmingham and then Manchester. Robert hated being away from Fairmans — the baby was due soon. On his arrival in Birmingham during the black-out he went for supper, and then couldn't find his way back to the hotel where he was staying. He wandered about half the night — no one would tell him the way as in wartime England strangers were to be treated as probable spies.

There was little question that this play was a far cry from *Play With Fire.* Huge audiences in Birmingham actually cheered, and all the critics called it 'brilliant'. The Opera House in Manchester was more like itself when they opened there. *The Guardian* reported that 'the laughter from last night's audience was pretty continuous.'

The Man Who Came To Dinner was to open on Thursday, December 4th, 1941 at the Savoy. Robert had lunch at Fairmans where the new stove had been installed and there were now shutters for the windows. There was also a nurse installed in readiness for the baby's arrival — but it was more imminent than anticipated. Robert left after lunch for the Savoy for his London first night and Joan left for the nursing home in Ascot for the arrival of her fiirst child. The first night went magnificently, though Robert's mind was more on his wife's confinement than the play. After the show he hurried down to Ascot and in the early hours of Friday morning his son was born. It was in the Royal Ascot Hotel where Robert had taken a room to be near Joan that he read the reviews of the play. The critics had again printed all the superlatives and predicted a very long run. At first Joan thought they might call the boy Simon — but Robert held out for Sheridan; being born on the first night it was only appropriate. Joan was apprehensive — it was quite usual, she thought, coming from a theatrical family, to name pets after characters in plays but she wasn't sure it was appropriate for children. Still, Sheridan it was and Alexander Woolcott agreed to be a godfather. Robert was dispatched to find dusting powder for Sheridan and apples for Joan in London; it was a difficult task but Fortnum and Mason obliged. Robert wrote to Joan from the Savoy that he had accomplished his task and that while on stage he would be thinking of her and 'wondering if the baby's nose is too big'. That weekend the Japanese attacked Pearl Harbour and the Americans were really in the war. Joan's brother wired 'Congratulations from me and all the little yellow people on our shores', but the cable was deemed unpatriotic and not delivered until after the war. The following Tuesday Sewell Stokes came to see the play. He was fire-watching but he could do it just as well from the Savoy. He also agreed to be a godfather and so did Peter Bull, now in the Navy.

Sheridan had arrived safely and the play was equally safely launched. Robert settled down to a long run. He commuted by train from Wargrave to Paddington each evening and then back again after the performance. Petrol rationing meant that he had to cycle the couple of miles to the station from the cottage. Peter Bull was soon on leave, back from Port Said. Robert got him a box at the Savoy and then perversely asked the cast to play completely to the other side of the house. Hysteria resulted all around, fuelled by the fact that Peter had brought Robert a pornographic book from his eastern travels which Robert in one scene handed to Coral, asking her to file it. Whenever he was home on leave Peter would travel down to Fairmans on the train with Robert. During the trip they played poker solidly and

Robert with Anna Neagle and Rex Harrison in I Live in Grosvenor Square

The First Gentleman

Robert and Annabel in Outcast of the Islands

Robert, Annabel, Joan, Wilton, Sheridan in Fairmans sitting room

Robert and Robert in A Likely Tale

Robert and Humphrey Bogart in Beat the Dev

Robert took to announcing just before vacating the carriage that Peter owed him something like eight thousand, four hundred and fifty pounds, just to see the look on the faces of the other passengers. And when he was at war, Peter was delighted to get the occasional £50 cheque from Robert to supplement his meagre allowance as an ordinary seaman.

The bombing had eased now but wartime restrictions made filming difficult still. Early in 1941 Twentieth Century Fox had decided to make a film in Britain about William Pitt, who at the age of 24 was Prime Minister of England during the Napoleonic Wars. Hollywood considered him to be the Winston Churchill of his age inciting the country against an earlier Hitler. The film was to be directed by Carol Reed from a story by Viscount Castleross but preliminaries were very slow and it was summer before it went into production. Robert Donat was playing Pitt and insisted on a closed set at Shepherd's Bush studios. 'I am not being temperamental,' he declared. 'I just cannot play a scene with a single pair of unnecessary eyes watching me. I am tougher than Garbo.'

It was a distinguished production. Robert played Pitt's opponent in the House of Commons, Charles James Fox, and John Mills played William Wilberforce. Phyllis Calvert was the love that Pitt sacrificed in the face of his duty. The film did not appear until the summer of '42. *The Man Who Came To Dinner* was still running at the Savoy. *The Young Mr Pitt* was lengthy in production and very expensive at £200,000 — it was one of the most costly films made in Britain — but it was a great success. The critics decided that it justified both the time and money — as a film and also as a piece of propaganda. 'The portrait of Fox,' Ernest Betts said in *The Sunday Express,* 'which Robert Morley gives is gloriously foxy, a delicious dose of political vinegar that sharpens the whole scene. When you listen to Mr Morley you realise what a pleasure it is to hear an actor speaking well.' *Variety* said: 'Robert Morley, who so frequently steals the show again, towers above the rest of the excellent cast.' And all the newspapers agreed, describing Robert's performance in terms that ranged from 'brilliant' through 'magnificent' — except the *Sunday Times*, which commented: 'I should not venture to pronounce on Robert Morley's performance as Fox — he is certainly first rate as Morley.'

After the filming was finished Robert's evenings were still occupied by *The Man Who Came To Dinner* and his afternoons were often taken up with bridge games, but the mornings he devoted to writing his latest play.

After *Play With Fire,* Ambrosine Phillpotts too had a great success in London in a play with Emlyn Williams called *The Morning Star*. But in 1942 she was pregnant and spent a good deal of time playing bridge with Robert. One day she didn't make the game. Her daughter Amanda had arrived three weeks early, and after the delivery she remembered the bridge date and rang Robert at the Savoy to apologise and explain. Robert sent round his play, *Staff Dance*. 'Here's a birthday present for Amanda,' the note said, 'I'd like you to play the part.' However, when she read it Ambrosine didn't like the play, and, never one to prevaricate, she told him so. Robert wasn't pleased. It was just about acceptable to criticize his performance — at times — but to criticize his writing was not allowed, and he didn't speak to her for months.

About six months later Coral Browne wanted to leave *The Man Who Came To Dinner*. There was a tour scheduled after the Savoy run and she didn't want to tour. Ambrosine was engaged to take over the part of the secretary. She rehearsed with the understudies and was supposed to have a proper rehearsal and about two more weeks to prepare before she actually took over, but Coral had an impacted wisdom tooth which was getting worse daily. Ambrosine was to step in on the Monday night and she was terrified. Not only did she have to push Robert about on the stage in a wheel-chair but there was also an enormous number of props to handle. Knowing well by this time Robert's mischievous sense of humour, especially in a long run, she was frightened that he would make matters even worse. He visited her dressing-room before the curtain went up, and she begged him not to play any tricks. 'Darling,' Robert said, 'would I?' But she didn't quite trust the twinkle in his eye. The play went at breakneck speed. Ambrosine, hands shaking with nerves, kept up. Robert could see she was handling it very well and he couldn't resist it. Ambrosine came to push the wheel-chair off stage and Robert put on the brake. 'Come on Sherry,' Ambrosine said, and gave a push, but the chair didn't move. She gave a tremendous shove, just as Robert took the brake off. She was so angry at the trick that she gave the chair another terrific shove and Robert took off at about sixty miles an hour heading straight for an enormous bust of him that was stored in the wings for another scene. Ambrosine watched in horror. 'If I've killed him,' she thought, 'Joan will kill me.' But Robert moved faster than anyone had ever seen and he was well out of the chair before the bust crashed down into it.

Robert enjoyed touring with Ambrosine. She could be counted on to know lots of people wherever they were as well as the best hotels, and besides she liked playing cards. Unfortunately that September in 1943, Joan had a miscarriage while the tour was in Blackpool and Robert couldn't get back to her. The tour went to Bristol, Leeds, Leicester, Manchester, Liverpool, Glasgow and Edinburgh, bringing laughter to war-weary England. In Edinburgh Robert found Henry Sherek, whose wartime duties centred in Scotland. After a couple of suppers that went on into the night, Sherek was exhausted but keen to do *The First Gentleman* — Robert wasn't sure any more. During most of the tour his main concern was with keeping certain members of the company sober (they were travelling 44 people!), and finding shoes for Sheridan. The food available varied from dried eggs — which Ambrosine pronounced too salty to be edible — to fresh salmon.

But the real horrors began when the company tour turned into an ENSA tour. It was very difficult to complain about facilities or anything else when touring under the aegis of ENSA. Wilfred Hyde White had tried it and found himself called into the army within three weeks. Robert wrote from Cardiff that it was 'rather what one might have expected, on the whole. Tiny stages and a pretty bad set of old flats and curtains. All much the same as Perranporth only a bit tattier.' Up and down Welsh mountains they bussed, playing to amazed and often dragooned service men. Robert tried to keep his mind off it by negotiating with Binkie Beaumont about producing *Staff Dance,* but the negotiations weren't going well either. Robert and Ambrosine returned from tea in a Welsh village one evening before the show to the tiny residential hotel they were staying in, to find in the lounge two members of the company stark naked, making love on the carpet in front of some rather startled locals. It was all too much. Finally they were released from their misery. One of the company developed chicken pox and the medical officer said it was too dangerous to visit the rest of the camps. Everyone went home and *The Man Who Came To Dinner* finally closed. It was very nearly 1944.

Robert had to go into the London Clinic. He had jaundice and a hernia as well. Binkie Beaumont had decided to produce *Staff Dance* for Tennant's. Jack Minster was to direct, Robert to star and the lady, the part Ambrosine had rejected, was to be Beatrice Lillie, the comedienne who had had great success in Charlot's revues and in America. But Bea was in a clinic in North London. She had not been her old self since her son was killed in the war in 1942. Every morning Mary Lynn Gordon, the stage manager, collected Bea from her nursing home and delivered her to Robert's, where they rehearsed the play in the basement. Bea nicknamed Jack Minster 'Laughing Jack' because of his permanent haunting gloom. His customary comment on anything Bea or Robert said was: 'I don't think that's funny.' Bea simply couldn't learn the moves or the lines. They were to open a pre-London tour in Oxford. Binkie despaired of ever getting her on the stage; she was pretty despairing herself. Privately, Binkie asked Ambrosine to stand by. 'Not on your life,' she said. Binkie pleaded. He made her a promise. If Bea played on the first night he'd release Ambrosine from the deal. So she learned the lines and was fitted for costumes, all in dead secrecy. On Sunday

Ambrosine travelled to Oxford with Joan in the guise of a friend simply coming to have a look. On the Monday she watched the dress rehearsal, desperately memorizing the moves, Bea wasn't there, and the understudy walked through it.

Bea Lillie's character didn't come on till the end of the first act. Ambrosine had to sit in the audience on the first night, completely made up and dressed for the stage. She sat next to Binkie on the gangway near the pass door. There was a light in the orchestra pit. If Bea couldn't make her entrance the light would go red. If she could, it would go green. The curtain went up, and Bea wasn't even in the theatre. Ambrosine sat transfixed through the performance, her eyes glued to the light. It was nearly time for Bea's entrance. Ambrosine prayed. The light came on — it was green. She got up and walked straight out of the theatre to the station, where she boarded a train for London. She had never felt so relieved. The tour was on the road.

Joan had chickens at Fairmans and took to posting eggs to the company because Bea ate little else and Robert said that they seemed to do her good. Robert in turn kept a look-out for suet which Joan couldn't get locally, but mostly he kept rewriting and redirecting the play. Although the box office receipts were good and the notices were fairly appreciative, it just didn't quite work. Bea complained that she didn't have any good lines. Robert complained that when she did she didn't say them, either because she forgot them or because she didn't trust them. The company went to Birmingham — and Glasgow, Aberdeen, Edinburgh, Newcastle, Liverpool, Derby, Leeds and Brighton, rewriting and re-rehearsing all the way — but the end came at Brighton. 'What is the advance booking like for London?' Robert asked Binkie. When Binkie told him, he said, 'That's not so much an advance as a retreat.' *Staff Dance* never made it to London. Ambrosine managed to restrain herself from saying, 'I told you so'. . . just.

Robert's next departure was to Totnes in Devon where he was scheduled to make a film for Herbert Wilcox, the

101

producer and director who helped found Elstree Studios. The film starred Anna Neagle, Wilcox's wife, with whom he had already made *Good Night Vienna* and *Nell Gwynne*. Robert was to play a duke who was also mayor of the town. He did a bit of research for the part at lunch with the actual town mayor, who wasn't a duke. Anna Neagle was to be his granddaughter, Rex Harrison an English soldier, and Dean Jagger an American soldier, both of whom were in competition for the hand of the beauteous English flower. To be a potential grandfather to Rex Harrison was rather daunting as Robert and Rex were almost the same age. But Robert was used to playing older parts. Only Anna Neagle and Dean Jagger were there when Robert arrived, so filming was a fair way off. 'Hurry up and wait' had been the motto not only for the army but also for a good deal of the film industry.

Herbert Wilcox walked around the town each morning deciding on location shots. Miss Neagle was constantly gracious, but Robert found her maddeningly enigmatic. Robert enjoys nothing so much as a good friendly argument. He may change sides in the middle of it, but to him conversation without a piquant touch is boring. This was not the style of the Wilcoxes and Robert turned to playing gin rummy with Dean Jagger. But the American was well-versed in the game and kept beating him — Robert found it necessary to lower the stakes. The morning newspapers often led Wilcox to alter the script in search of topicality. The film was eventually called *I Live In Grosvenor Square* (in America, *A Yank In London*). It was not a great success. *The New Statesman* said: 'It repeats the parody of English life offered by *Mrs Minniver* and *The White Cliffs Of Dover*', and all the papers agreed that an English production company should have known better. But by the time it opened in London Robert was back in the West End with a success.

It was 1945 now, and the war was coming to an end. Evelyn Waugh's *Brideshead Revisited* was published. It is one of the few books that Robert has been seen actually to read from cover to cover. He reads a lot, but generally begins somewhere in the middle, and skips back and forth until the meat is extracted.

Robert thought *The First Gentleman* a good play but there is no play which to his mind can't be improved by a bit of rewriting. It was to be a long tour with a good deal of rewriting. But before beginning rehearsals Robert found himself in a nursing home again, this time in Bournemouth. It was a quinsy throat again. The room was very comfortable, overlooking the bay, but he didn't care much for having penicillin jabs every two hours, especially as he had had to fight for them. The local doctor had said he couldn't have any, but Robert insisted that he had to have the new wonder drug he had read about. The specialist arrived and prescribed it after commenting that Robert's tonsils were 'a disgrace to the stage'.

The First Gentleman opened at the Opera House in Manchester on April 2nd. Norman Marshall was directing and Wendy Hiller played Charlotte, the Prince Regent's daughter. It was a massive play covering five years and had four large scene changes. But according to the Manchester critics it was Robert's evening. 'It would indeed be no cause for wonder if the author had written his play around this most polished actor,' said the *News Chronicle,* which was rather surprising as almost every actor in London had turned it down. The *Manchester Evening News* summed it up: 'If you take away the Prince Regent you have nothing left. The outcome is a magnificent monologue by Robert Morley — a performance of such virtuosity in the grand, or Morley manner, that it suggests the sub title: *The Man Who Came To Dinner In The Brighton Pavilion.'* Even before reading the reviews, the company met in Robert's room at the Midland Hotel. There was no doubt in anyone's mind there would have to be some rewriting — in fact a good deal of it.

Robert worked very hard over the weekend, and taking advantage of Ginsbury's absence, entirely rewrote the first half hour of the play. He put a new scene into the second act and reworked most of the exit lines. They decided to have it typed on Monday in Edinburgh but when they arrived they found that it was a Scottish Bank Holiday and there were no typing offices open. They were to play at the King's Theatre in Edinburgh, owned by the Wyndham chain. Alec Cruickshank was the manager and he said they could use the offices there and do the typing themselves. Beforehand he gave them lunch and then decided to give Robert a tour of the offices. The Wyndham organization owned numbers of theatres around the country and often organized their own tours. In a moment of madness Cruickshank showed Robert the file Wyndham's kept on artists they employed. Robert found it riveting. He took out one file on a famous touring performer: 'Asks £350,' it said, 'worth £150 — definitely going off.' Another said simply 'Bad worker'. Robert could easily have spent the day there, but he tore himself away and, meeting up again with his producer, Henry Sherek and his wife Pamela, ushered them into a room which housed at least a dozen typewriters. He handed out bits of paper and they set to work. None of them could type properly so it was very slow going, pecking away with a couple of fingers each. Their industry pleased Robert. 'You know,' he told Sherek delightedly, 'Binkie Beaumont would never do this.'

Norman Ginsbury arrived in Edinburgh that week and viewed the now very rewritten play. Robert thought he took it quite well. 'I'm confident,' he told Robert, 'I can make something of it when I get back to London.' Robert thought he had already made something of it himself.

Gladys Cooper arrived at Fairmans while Robert was on tour. Joan reported that she seemed quite pleased with her first grandchild, whom she was seeing for the first time although Sheridan was nearly four. The war and her Hollywood contract had kept her on the other side of the Atlantic but now she was over for a couple of months making an American film. Also at Fairmans the construction of a small wooden house at the end of the garden was in progress. It was to be Robert's study. Once again he was determined to give up acting and concentrate on writing. George Bernard Shaw had a little house at the bottom of his garden — Robert would have one too.

Although Ginsbury wasn't arguing that much with

104

Robert, he was furious with Sherek. Robert kept assuring his producer that he would handle Ginsbury. On the tour, which covered Newcastle, Coventry, Brighton and sundry other cities, Robert developed his usual pre-London cold. Wendy Hiller mixed him some herb tea and left it in his bedroom with a large notice on it saying 'Drink me'. He did, and woke at three in the morning with the most awful stomach ache. He spent the rest of the night cursing her. In the morning Wendy came in to see how he was and he told her in no uncertain terms what she had done to him.

'Oh dear, dear', she said, 'How angry Ronald [her husband] will be.'

'Why?' Robert asked. Whatever did it have to do with him?

'Well, you see I did the same thing to him before we were married. He was very bad and had to lie down in Harrods.'

The company took to calling Wendy 'Miss Borgia'. But in the end Robert decided it had done him some good. He was so busy worrying about his stomach ache that his cold disappeared.

All through the tour rewriting and rehearsing continued. At last Sherek decided that it all worked. It was time to bring the play to London. But there was a major problem. He was getting solicitors' letters from the author. Ginsbury had put an injunction on the play. He wasn't pleased with the changes, and an injunction meant that Sherek couldn't present the play in London without the author's approval. But Robert's contract gave him script approval and he wasn't about to change it back to its original form. It was a stalemate. Perhaps all that work had been for nothing. Robert didn't mind particularly. A holiday would be nice. He hadn't had one for five years. Besides, he wanted to get on with writing a play that had been in his mind for some time.

The law, however, was on Sherek's side. The injunction, counsel decided, was unenforceable. In the end Ginsbury withdrew it before the first night. Then another problem cropped up. There wasn't a theatre available in the West End. Finally Sherek was offered the New Theatre, but only for seven weeks. It had become the home of the Old Vic

Company and he could only have it for the summer between their Shakespearean seasons. He took it. *The First Gentleman* opened at the New Theatre on July 17th, 1945. 'Robert Morley's Prince Regent,' said the *Sunday Express,* 'strides through casting pavilions of hypocrisy, scattering pearls of wisdom to high and low — a beautiful performance you can actually hear. So, too, is the fiery Charlotte of Wendy Hiller and Amy Frank's Princess of Wales. This is elegance, wit and charm.' James Agate in the *Sunday Times* called the play 'good theatre and always and at all times excellent entertainment'. The play was a hit. It would mean a long run — if they could find a theatre.

Winston Churchill celebrated VJ day by going to the theatre with his wife and daughter Sarah to see *The First Gentleman.* As he arrived the whole audience stood, cheered and sang, 'For he's a jolly good fellow'. At the curtain call Robert made a speech announcing that 'The first gentleman of Europe is in the stalls.' Churchill sent word backstage that he had been very touched by Robert's words about him — but he didn't mention Robert's performance.

At the end of August the company transferred to the Savoy Theatre and settled there for about eighteen months.

During the run of *The First Gentleman* Henry Sherek kept on at Robert to write his play, which at the time he called *My Son, Edward.* He had begun the idea one day when he was bathing Sheridan. What Robert felt was the mixture of pride and humility that every father feels — a sensation which in his case he called a mixture of smugness and apprehension. He decided that what he wanted to say in his play was that a child who can quote his father when he grows up is likely to be happier than one who can't or doesn't choose to. Sherek thought it was a wonderful idea. But Robert, being a gregarious man, much preferred a good lunch, a day at the races, or a bit of gambling to agonizing over a typewriter.

While playing the Prince Regent Robert carried on a continuous bridge game. Another actor would finish his hand if he was called onto the stage and signal the results to him from the wings. But on matinee days Henry Sherek would arrive and they played between the shows. Robert would come off stage from the afternoon performance to find Henry already at his place. One day Sherek wasn't there at the appointed time. Robert found an understudy to take over the empty seat, and had just completed the first deal when Henry appeared breathlessly at the dressing-room door. He was a very big man — bigger than Robert, and so he was often breathless, but this time more so than usual. There then ensued one of those ridiculous quarrels for the sake of argument that Robert sometimes indulges in — especially when he is feeling a bit restless in a long run. Henry said he'd take over the hand and asked the understudy to move.

'Just a moment,' Robert said, 'you were late — now you'll have to cut in after the rubber.'

Henry turned purple. 'Do you realize,' he shouted, 'that I have come all the way from Edinburgh, where I had a production running that I should have seen the matinee of, so that I shouldn't let you blasted four down? It's not my fault that the train was late. If I don't play now I'll never play bridge with any of you again.'

Robert found it enormous fun. 'That's up to you,' he said coolly. 'Meantime, you're delaying the rubber.'

Henry answered, school-boy fashion, 'Besides, I've sprained my ankle coming downstairs and it's beginning to swell.'

A play for sympathy only increased Robert's obstinacy. The understudy, not caring for the scene, had handed the cards to Sherek. 'New deal,' Robert shouted, 'and give the cards back, Henry.' Henry couldn't believe it. 'Do you mean that?' Robert assured him he did. Henry declared it was the end. He wasn't going to be treated like that. 'Never again,' he told Robert as he hobbled out. 'I shan't forget this.'

Robert was still wondering if he had gone too far when he looked up and saw that Henry was back in the room. He had calmed down. 'I suppose I might as well cut in,' he said quietly. 'I have come all the way from Edinburgh and I don't think I can get up the stairs with my ankle.' The matinee day games continued.

107

Noel Langley, the scriptwriter whom Robert had met in Hollywood, came to see the play. Robert told him about *My Son, Edward* and they agreed to work on it together — but it became a very separate togetherness. Without a co-writer, Robert would never get down to it. He needed the discipline of someone waiting for a script, and really preferred it if all the actors were standing on stage waiting for their lines. Otherwise life intervened and the lines didn't get written. Langley agreed to go down to Fairmans to spend the weekend. But he made certain provisions. He would move into Robert's study — the tiny hut at the bottom of the garden. He would remain there undisturbed. His meals were to be sent in and he would sleep there. It was agreed. Outside Robert prowled around the garden, peeping through the windows, but left Langley alone. On Monday morning Robert went to investigate. He found that Langley had gone and left a pile of typewritten pages. *Edward, My Son* was underway. Now Robert could get on with the fiddling, juxtaposing and rewriting. His idea was at last down in black and white and existed.

Annabel, Robert and Joan's only daughter, was born during the run of *The First Gentleman*. She came early, on June 10th, 1946, at home and Robert was amazed to find that her legs were no thicker than his finger — which was not too alarming considering the size of Robert's fingers. But she was under four pounds and there was no incubator at Fairmans. The nurse improvised and put the cot up against the heated cupboard where the linen was kept. Annabel thrived, but Robert was too terrified to touch her. He thought she would snap. 'One of us,' he kept thinking, 'is the wrong size.'

Everyone came to see *The First Gentleman*. The papers reported that Princess Elizabeth and Mary Pickford attended the same night. And Robert finished *Edward, My Son*. He had no intention of playing in it himself. He was quite happy at the Savoy and Henry Sherek was working on a deal to take *The First Gentleman* to New York. Moreover Robert liked the idea of becoming a full-time writer and not having to act every night. He had rather promised the play to

Henry Sherek, but Peter Bull had just lost a lot of money on a production and Robert thought it might help him out if he co-produced. Peter didn't like it very much but Robert asked him to take it to a couple of actors. There was a part in it for Pauline Letts, the girl from Perranporth. Both Peter and Robert felt guilty that she hadn't played *Goodness How Sad* in London. As for the lead — well, Peter took it personally to Robert Donat and to Clive Brook, who both said no. They thought the character of Lord Holt too unsympathetic. Robert was still determined not to play Holt himself. The play, he knew, had a life of its own and the part entailed a great many changes and a good deal of sheer physical energy. He decided that Ian Hunter was the man to play Holt. Ian had been on the London stage since 1921. He had gone to Hollywood in 1935 and appeared in innumerable films before returning for the war. He hadn't been on the stage in the West End for more than ten years when Sherek was persuaded by Robert that he should have the part. The three of them lunched at the Ecu de France and finalized the deal. After lunch, outside on the curb, Robert and Henry shook hands with Ian and bid him good-bye. Then as Robert watched him disappear around the corner with the script and the contract, he realized that Ian would never have the verve and attack which the role required.

'I have,' Robert told Sherek, 'written the little play and cut its bloody throat.'

'Then you'll do it after all?' Sherek asked.

'I suppose so, but what about Ian?'

'There is always the billing clause,' Sherek replied, which meant that he could make it so difficult, as the producer, for Hunter that he would have to quit. But instead Robert told Ian that they had had second thoughts, and being a very good-natured person he withdrew.

Robert began to make immediate plans for the production and for closing the run of *The First Gentleman*. It closed on November 16th 1946 having been one of London's biggest successes, seen by more than 500,000 people. Robert went to Monte Carlo for a holiday at last.

CHAPTER EIGHT

HENRY SHEREK, WHO HAD WEATHERED both the tour and the success of *The First Gentleman* was to present *Edward, My Son* in conjunction with Gilbert Miller, who had presented *Oscar Wilde* in New York. Sherek wanted their old friend Norman Marshall to direct it, but Norman had taken the Arts Theatre for a season and wasn't available. Peter Ashmore was the next choice. Ashmore had been working at the Playhouse, Oxford and Robert had seen his production of *Caste* at the Lyric, Hammersmith. He thought it very good indeed, so Ashmore drove down to Wargrave one snowy evening to talk to Robert about the play. They talked for hours, but still Robert wasn't completely sure. *Edward* was very precious to him. He was loath to trust it to anyone. About midnight Peter left. He was back on the doorstep in half an hour. He was very sorry to disturb them but could he possibly borrow a flashlight? He had had a flat tyre about a mile down the road.

Robert looked out at the snow. He was in his pyjamas. Rather reluctantly he offered to help Peter with the tyre. 'Oh, no,' Peter assured him, all he needed was a flashlight. Robert found him one, climbed the stairs and went back to bed. 'If he gets out of this one on his own,' he said to Joan as he slid between the sheets, 'he must be exactly the right person to direct *Edward.*' He was. That settled, they got on with casting. Robert had written the part of Holt's wife with Pauline Letts in mind, but the day she went for an interview

110

with Sherek was also the day she discovered that she was pregnant. Peggy Ashcroft rather hesitantly agreed to play the part of Evelyn Holt, Edward's mother, who gradually in depression and despair turns to drink. It was a departure from the kind of roles she was used to, and she stipulated that though she would do the tour, she reserved the right not to open in London. Sherek agreed.

He was very pleased to have her and felt that as soon as she got her teeth into the part she would stay. There is, however, another important female part in *Edward,* that of Eileen Perry, Holt's secretary and mistress. Both Robert and Henry Sherek were keen to have Irene Worth play it, but she was involved in a tour of *The Play's The Thing,* and Leueen McGrath became Eileen Perry. Rehearsals were not easy. Robert was constantly rewriting, rethinking, and Peggy Ashcroft cried so hard at her imagined inability and failure in the part that she was always rushing to her dressing-room to sob her heart out. Robert asked the advice of her former colleagues. 'The first thing to do,' he was told, 'is to get the key to her dressing-room each morning before she does.' Finally Ted Upton went to Robert with a warning: 'If the weeping and gnashing of teeth continues on her part and the uncertainty on yours, you are all going to lose a lot of money.' That shook Robert. He rang Ambrosine and extracted a promise from her that she would stand by in case she was needed. Then he bought a huge bunch of roses and went to Peggy's Highgate house.

'I've come,' he told her, 'to set you free. You're not letting me down. I have someone who will open in Leeds. Here is your chance to get out, forget the whole thing. Give up the part.'

'Are you sure,' Peggy asked him. 'I won't be letting you down?'

'Sure,' Robert replied hoping very much the ploy would work. He didn't want to lose her. 'Only remember,' he continued, 'that once you have chucked you will go on chucking. You will give up the next part and the one after that.' This Robert firmly believed. If an actor once gives up a part he is rehearsing his confidence never recovers. Being sacked is a different thing.

Peggy was back in the morning and the play took shape.

It was March, 1947 in Leeds when Robert first stepped in front of the curtain in a long black overcoat with an astrakhan collar. He wore a black homburg over his greyed hair. One spotlight lit him as he fixed the audience with his eyes and addressed them:

'My name, ladies and gentlemen, is Holt, Lord Holt. You'll have seen my pictures in the paper quite a lot these last few years. When you get home you can look me up in *Who's Who*. If you happen to have one. It won't tell you everything about me but there's quite a lot there now, nearly half a page. It will tell you where I was born and where I went to school, whom I married and what offices I've held under the crown. It will tell you some of the committees I've served on in my time. I'm not asked to serve on many now — but it won't tell you that I happen to own this theatre — I thought that would surprise you. It won't tell you that I am proprietor of a great national newspaper, that I'm Hythes Lager Beer and Hungerford's Stores and the Brewster Match Company, that I control Provenders and through it six of the eight big biscuit firms in this country.

'I am telling you all this, not because I want to boast, but because I want to establish some contact with you. Just because you read my papers or eat my biscuits or sit in my theatre it doesn't mean that you have to like me — or I you for that matter. But it does mean that our lives, like a lot of other people's lives, have already crossed to a certain extent. That is why I should value your opinion. What would you have done on that foggy February morning? Would you have gone on or gone back? I wonder.

'The trouble is, of course, that none of you knew Edward, and now he's dead and it's too late. Mind you, you'll meet other people here tonight who are dead. Evelyn, for instance, and Harry Soames and Hanray. But with Edward it's different because he was my son. My only son. He was twenty-three when he was killed, a pleasant-looking boy

112

with charming manners and a lovely smile. That doesn't add up to very much, does it, but it's all I can tell you about him now. Later on— well, you'll see for yourselves how it was.

'Supposing we make a start. It is November 11th, 1919. A year ago today the Armistice was signed and my son was born. We live in a little maisonette in Brighton, but just before we begin I think I'll get Evelyn to tell you a little more about Edward. You see, for the first year she really knew him better than I did.'

The light dimmed, Robert exited, and the audience settled back for a three-act play with more than ten scenes. When Robert finally came off the stage, to shouts of 'Bravo', Sherek, waiting in the wings, informed him nervously that it had run for over three-and-a-half hours. Robert was surprised. He could still hear the audience shouting with delight. 'Do you know, this is the first time I've appeared in a play as long as that.'

By the second night an entire scene had been cut, the set changes speeded up, and it ran just three hours. But that was just the beginning of the cutting, rewriting and rehearsals that went on for the ten-week tour. Peter Ashmore was an enormous help. Robert felt that the director understood the play almost better than he did himself and, more important, he loved it as much. He knew which scenes Robert should keep working on and which ones to leave alone.

The provinces were encouraging. Robert got the best receptions he had ever had from the audiences. Peggy Ashcroft was still a bit apprehensive. She found it difficult to get into the character of the disillusioned wife and mother. Robert had admitted that it was the one part he had rather underwritten knowing that Peggy would make something of it — and she did magnificently. By the time they reached Newcastle she had cheered up. A man in the stalls leaped to his feet at the end of the performance and shouted 'You've got a winner.'

Robert had his 39th birthday at home with Joan and the children. *Edward, My Son* opened at His Majesty's Theatre in the Haymarket on May 30th. The night before there was an interminable lighting and dress rehearsal. Robert ducked the third act altogether and took his place beside Sherek in the dress circle. He had removed all his make-up.

'What are you doing?' Henry asked.

'Going home,' Robert told him. 'I have a first night tomorrow.'

Henry Sherek was still fussing about the last scene in which Robert came out of the play and addressed the audience. Sherek had never liked it but Robert refused to change it.

The newspapers the next day declared the play a success. Critic Elspeth Grant said: 'This is a compelling play about a father who for the sake of his son founded a fortune by incendiarism, provided education through blackmail and as time went on betrayed his partner, his wife, the girl who loved his son and his country.' All the writers seemed fascinated that Edward, the pivotal character of the play, was never seen. And from the notices, Peggy Ashcroft had been right to stick with *Edward* despite her doubts. Beverly Baxter wrote in the *Evening Standard:* 'For some years I have watched Miss Ashcroft in sweetly pretty parts and could never reach the ecstasy of appreciation shown by some other critics. But in this play, as the faithful wife of the self-made domineering peer who tries to drown her memories in black-market whiskey she emerges as an actress of astonishing gifts.'

The reviews were generally good but not outstanding. A couple of the critics singled out the last scene that Sherek objected to. 'It ends in 1947, during the fuel cuts, with Morley planning to abandon his country taking his grandson with him. A friend in the scene suggests that he step out of character, address the audience and ask: "Shall I do it?" Morley actually asks the question,' the *Daily Express* reported, 'but before anyone can answer he makes his own decision. It was a smart-aleck piece of theatre that put the only flaw in a brilliantly successful play.'

That night Sherek arrived in Robert's dressing-room as he was making up. 'It's obvious,' he told him, 'that I was right about the last scene. It could be fixed tonight.' Robert didn't want to discuss it. 'Open that letter on my table will you,' he said, 'my fingers are all sticky from the make-up.' The letter was from Noel Langley, who had been in front on the first night. He, too, thought the scene should be changed. Robert sensed a plot. He had always considered it a virtue to be blind to the faults of his children and those he loved — and *Edward* was a much loved child. He could not bear any criticism. His mouth tightened and his eyes blazed as he accused Sherek of collusion.

Henry told him that he hadn't even spoken to Langley.

'I don't believe it,' Robert shouted in rage. Sherek thought for a moment that he was going to be hit, but Robert picked up a small comb which was lying on his dressing-table and hurled it at him — as well as he could hurl a tiny comb. It fluttered and fell to the floor. Sherek picked it up and threw it back. These two enormous men stood there for minutes throwing this insignificant thing back and forth until the ridiculousness of the situation struck them, and they collapsed in fits of laughter. Robert snatched the envelope and began writing a new end to the play. He would finish the last scene without talking to the audience. Then the curtain would fall and he would come in front of it as he had at the beginning — dressed in the overcoat and homburg — one spotlight on his face.

'Well, ladies and gentlemen, that's how it all happened, more or less. I wonder what you would have done if you'd been me on that foggy February morning at the station. Would you have gone on or would you have turned back for them? I know what I did. Well, that's all, ladies and gentlemen. Look after yourselves. The way things are in this world, nobody else will.'

Then Robert lifted his hat and waved a cheerful farewell.

That was it. The critics from the Sunday and weekly papers were in the audience the second night and they were well pleased. Harold Hobson reported: *Edward, My Son* is a very accomplished piece of playwriting. Its unity of theme holds it together in spite of its episodic nature. It is witty, its curtain and exit lines are pungent and slick. It is admirably played.'

Despite the notices, the audiences built only slowly. For a while Sherek was losing money but he had faith that it was only temporary. But Jack Hylton, from whom he leased His Majesty's Theatre, didn't, and threatened to give him four weeks' notice to quit the theatre. Sherek booked the Lyric and decided to give notice himself in case Hylton didn't, and he would be stuck with two theatres for one play which was losing money. In the end they exchanged their letters simultaneously. By some stroke of magic, as soon as the decision to leave that theatre in four weeks was made, business shot up. The house was full every night and the transfer to the Lyric in Shaftesbury Avenue on September 29th was a great success.

Joan had taken the children for a seaside holiday at Frinton in August. Robert commuted down there on Saturday after the show to spend Sunday with the family, but the rest of the time he stayed in London. There was no point to going back to Wargrave each evening if the family was away. He was getting the play ready for the printed version and found it very tedious copying all the moves into the text. But he wasn't finding the offers for the film rights to *Edward, My Son* at all tiresome. Herbert Wilcox wanted the property for Anna Neagle and Michael Wilding and was offering £20,000 and a share of the profits. Robert just couldn't see that couple making a success of the play. He turned the offer down, which was just as well because MGM had their eye on it too, as a vehicle for their big star, Spencer Tracy. They more than doubled Wilcox's offer, and *Edward, My Son* was sold for a record sum in 1947.

Robert was walking down Jermyn Street one evening on his way to the theatre when he spotted Llewellyn Rees, whom he hadn't seen since the beginning of the war when he was on the Council of Equity.

'Hello,' Robert called, 'I haven't seen you for ages. How are you?'

'Oh, I'm all right,' Llewellyn said. 'Most of my friends think I'm dead.'

'Surely not if they look closely.' Robert was so pleased with his line he made Llewellyn come to the theatre with him so they could repeat it in front of Peggy Ashcroft.

Minor problems cropped up during the run. One of the subsidiary characters was called Montague Burton. There was, living in Ascot, a Sir Montague Burton, the head of a very large chain of tailoring shops. Someone pointed out to him that his name was being taken in vain each evening in the West End and he duly wrote to Robert expressing his displeasure. Robert pointed out that almost every name belonged to someone and he couldn't very well call his characters AZ or XY. He was involved at that moment in raising money for a children's charity and he added in his reply that if Sir Montague Burton cared to send him a cheque for £250 he would see what he could do. The cheque arrived and Robert dropped the Montague, referring to the character only as Burton.

The play settled into a long run and celebrities began turning up in the audience. Robert was delighted to find Orson Welles there one night and on another occasion Queen Mary, who received him during one of the intervals. Robert and Peggy Ashcroft were given the Ellen Terry Award for best actor and actress in 1947 and MGM arrived in England to film Spencer Tracy and Deborah Kerr in the play, adapted for the screen by Donald Ogden Stewart. George Cukor was directing. They had agreed that the film wouldn't be released until 1949 so as not to interfere with the Broadway production.

That summer found the Morleys packing up. It was to be a major tour, New York and then Australia — but first a visit to Gladys in Hollywood and a holiday there. It would be years before they returned, and who knows, Robert thought, they just might stay in America.

Edward, My Son was to go on running at the Lyric. John Clements took over Robert's part and Pauline Letts, who had been delivered of a daughter the summer before, took over from Peggy Ashcroft. Peggy needed some time off from it before travelling to America with the company. And Irene Worth was finally playing the secretary since Leueen McGrath was also going to America.

Joan found a new nanny, Nancy Stubbs, because her old one couldn't face going to America. Robert's sister Margaret was going to come and live at Fairmans with her two daughters and look after the house and the dogs. Robert's mother had moved into a small flat quite near the house. It was all organized. Robert, Joan, the two children and the nurse were to sail on the *Queen Elizabeth* in late July then take a train across America to California. It was a major operation but well-planned. Then Sheridan came down with chicken pox. As there is a two to three week incubation period, they realized that they would be mid-trip when Annabel, just two, succumbed inevitably to the disease. They quickly packed her off with Nancy by air to California while they sailed with all the luggage and Sheridan.

Graham Greene was on board, as was Carol Reed and his family. They were on their way to America to make *The Third Man*. Robert found them congenial company. As Greene was a quiet, shy man, rather reclusive and frightened of children, Robert rather bullied him into organizing games for the children. It would do him good, Robert assured him.

They had never seen Gladys's house on Napoli Drive in Pacific Palisades, and found it delightful. It looked out over a golf course and beyond it to the sea. They had the house to themselves as Gladys had built a tiny cottage with a swimming pool next door for herself. They arrived on the Friday morning and slept most of the day. Annabel had indeed developed chicken pox the week before they arrived. The spots were just beginning to fade.

Rex Harrison and Lilli Palmer came to dinner one Saturday night. They had recovered from the flight by then, but Robert found Rex rather a bit subdued. It wasn't surprising. Only a month before he had been to Carole Landis's funeral. Carole was a beautiful and spirited actress with whom Rex had been having an affair. One night he had

118

gone to her home to find that she was dead, having taken an overdose of sleeping pills and a good deal of alcohol. The press had had a field day with the story.

The California weather was perfect that summer. Daytimes were spent either in the swimming pool or a few steps away on the beach. There were parties in the evening, at which Robert often found himself defending Atlee's Labour government. For some reason the Hollywood moguls felt that the British government had something to do with the film slump. Graham Greene had arrived on the West Coast, after a delay in New York. He had brought his passport but neglected to get a visa. Robert took him off to show him Chinatown. There were days racing at La Jolla and drives out into the desert, trips to Catalina Island, and Robert began to regret having to go to New York at all. Life was just too comfortable. Gladys had been promising for years that she would introduce Robert to Greta Garbo. Finally, on September 4th, she gave a lunch party. Constance Collier, Ethel Barrymore, Edmund Gwenn and Arthur Wimperis were there, and so was Garbo. Robert wasn't disappointed. She was everything he had imagined she would be. She looked wonderful and was charming, very gay and amusing.

Meanwhile Henry Sherek and Gilbert Miller were pacing the floor in New York waiting for Robert to arrive. Broadway success for *Edward, My Son* was by no means assured. There was a good deal of anti-British feeling in New York that autumn, especially among the Jewish community, which mattered a lot to the success of any play. The tension in Palestine was the cause. A successful show arriving from England usually meant a good deal of advance booking. There was very little.

Henry Sherek had felt somehow that rehearsals in New York would be more exciting than they had been in London. They were necessary because so many members of the cast were new, and besides they had to slow it down so that it would be comprehensible to the American ear. But rehearsals seemed much the same. The stage looked bare

119

and ugly with only one light which made the actors look awful. Peggy Ashcroft sat at the back of the stage writing letters when she wasn't needed, and he thought Robert wandered through it all as if he didn't have a care in the world.

Robert had left the family in California and flown to New York. It wasn't, he thought, as he had left it ten years before. It seemed much tougher and cruder and he found that prices had risen incredibly. A pound for a steak dinner! He rang Joan most evenings. He was staying at the Hotel Maurice and not even contemplating a permanent residence. After all, the play might flop.

They had a pre-Broadway try out at the Shubert Theatre in New Haven, Connecticut and took seven curtain calls. 'And there might have been more bows,' Fred Russell reported in *The Bridgeport Post,* 'if Robert Morley, the star, had not stepped forward after the seventh and thanked the audience for its reponse.'

Edward, My Son opened at the Martin Beck Theatre on Thursday, September 30th, 1948. It had been a disastrous season so far with shows closing as fast as they opened. *Sunadown Beach* ran for seven performances; *Hilarities* for fourteen; *Heaven On Earth* — twelve; *A Story For Strangers* — seven; *Grandma's Diary* — six; *Town House* — twelve and *Time For Elizabeth* — eight. Was Robert about to follow suit? Gladys and Joan flew in for the first night. It was a surprise. Gladys was making *The Secret Garden* and didn't know until the last minute if she could get away from the filming — and Joan certainly wasn't going to fly by herself.

It was a massive New York first night such as only Broadway can provide. Celeste Holm, Cole Porter, Gertrude Lawrence, William Saroyan and Lillian Hellman were there. And at the final curtain cheers went up. The drought was over; Broadway had a hit at last.

'How do you think it went?' Robert asked Joan when she came backstage. She looked amazed at the question. 'Well, it went very much as it has been going for two years.' Joan never concerned herself with Robert's work. She never became the wife who sits in the dressing-room waiting for the curtain to fall; nor did she ever count the number of people in the audience. Gladys gave a party at the Blue Angel. Sherek, Miller and Morley — none of them small men — took up most of the room in the tiny restaurant. The next day the critics announced unanimously what everyone in the audience that night had felt — at last, a wonderful show. Three of them actually used the word 'magnificent' which Sherek and Miller lost no time in hanging outside the theatre. Joan stayed till the Monday and they went house-hunting. They could obviously stay on Broadway as long as they wanted to. New York was pleased to have them. Robert decided maybe it was still a lovely place.

Just as Joan was leaving for the airport they found an apartment on Park Avenue that would do. It had three bedrooms, two maid's rooms, a big drawing-room and a dining-room. A Swedish daily help and a Scottish cook went with it. It was near the park and a school which Wendy Hiller had said would do for Sheridan. Joan thought they might have done better, it was fearfully expensive, but Robert wanted to settle it before she went back to California. Robert planned to move in on October 20th and Joan would come at the end of the month with Nancy and the children. In the meantime Robert had to find a replacement for Peggy Ashcroft, who was leaving at the end of November. He tried Celia Johnson, without success, and considered Deborah Kerr who had made the film with Spencer Tracy. Nothing was decided when the director, Peter Ashmore, returned to England on the *Queen Elizabeth*.

There were lots of radio shows and interviews for Robert to do. He hoped to get the publicity over with before Joan and the children arrived. Richard Maney was again his press agent — the man who had steered him through his first success in *Oscar Wilde*. (He had told him exactly what to do and how to behave. 'When Mrs Vanderbilt asks you to tea,' he said, 'you go and no bull shit.') He got the play ready for the American publishers and began writing a new play for Gladys. Spencer Tracy came to see *Edward* for the first time

121

and told Robert that he thought they had made a mess of the film. Because of the censor in America they had had to change the ending and send Holt to prison, which made it all rather gloomy. Robert was working quite hard rehearsing Meg Mundy who he had decided might be able to take over from Peggy Ashcroft. He was delighted by the stars coming nightly to see the show — Dorothy Gish, Charles Boyer and Jennifer Jones on one night.

Robert was fascinated by the American election. Gilbert Miller had told him that the chances of Truman beating Dewey were 50-1 against and Miller had placed a substantial bet along those lines. On election night Robert stayed at the 21 Club until two in the morning, watching the results coming in on television. Miller was feeling rather sick the next day. But Robert decided that Truman, who had been handicapped by having no support from his congress for the past two years, would make some progress. Anyway, he thought him a better choice from the English point of view.

Rehearsals with Meg Mundy were agony. Everyone kept telling Robert that American actresses built from beneath and that he wasn't to expect a performance until opening night. Then suddenly, five days before she was due to take over, the stage manager who was watching from the row behind Robert in the stalls leant forward and said: 'She's never going to get it, you know.'

'No,' Robert told him, 'I didn't know.' And he rushed on the stage in a panic. 'In this part,' he told Meg, 'you're not only a mouse, you are a so and so mouse.' The bullying didn't work and that afternoon they had no one to play the part. Adrianne Allen agreed to take over. It meant rehearsing all over again but Robert felt sure that with Adrianne's experience she would be fine. She came straight from the boat to the first rehearsal. 'Just tell me where you would like me to stand.' she said.

Joan left California on November 13th for the three-and-a-half day journey by train to New York. Robert met them at the station, pleased to find they had survived the journey and that he could at last understand Annabel, whose baby talk had matured considerably. Joan discovered that the Scots cook who came with the apartment and whom Robert had been so pleased with for nearly a month not only drank a good deal but also had left the kitchen absolutely filthy. She was dismissed, and a rather ancient but reliable English cook was installed after Joan, Nancy and the Swedish daily had spent three days cleaning up. Sheridan was enrolled in the progressive school Wendy had recommended, and they all settled down to the winter in New York.

Edward, My Son was playing every performance to capacity standing room. Moreover, the Martin Beck Theatre became the centre of theatrical social life that season. Robert took to having tea served in his dressing-room on matinee days. Adrianne Allen baked the cakes and they invited people from other shows running on Broadway. Rex Harrison was playing Henry VIII in *Anne Of A Thousand Days* and he came frequently, as did visiting British actors and anyone Robert felt like inviting. Invitations were prized as it was *the* place to be — as was Sardi's, especially when Robert practically took it over for his supper parties.

Gladys came from California to spend Christmas with them — and it was a brilliant Christmas, especially after the rather muted celebrations in wartime and early post-war England. The giant Christmas tree went up outside Radio City and smaller decorated trees lined Park Avenue. Even with the whirl of social activity Robert managed to fit in a good deal of work as well as the play. In January he did his first television programme. He approached it with trepidation. There was a psychiatrist and a drama critic who were to debate what Robert was *really* saying in *Edward, My Son*. He listened quietly and then contradicted them both. Still, he found having three cameras constantly on him rather off-putting. He would have to learn to overcome his nerves, he decided. Television seemed a fascinating medium. In 1948, however, he still preferred the radio and was happier doing *The Late George Apley* for the Lux Radio Theatre than he was appearing on television. A publisher took him out to lunch and offered to publish his

123

autobiography which, very flattered, Robert duly began to write. He finished one chapter. There was so much to do in New York it was impossible to sit down and write. Parties intervened. Beatrice Lillie had a lovely flat in New York overlooking the river, where she often had supper parties for him.She was trying to talk Robert into doing *Staff Dance* in America, but he thought not. They hadn't managed to make it work for London and he didn't envisage much success with it on Broadway.

Edward continued to be *the* show to see. Helen Keller came with a nurse-companion who translated everything into a touch sign language for her, and the King and Queen of Yugoslavia asked Joan to get them seats because, being short of dollars, they couldn't afford the inflated prices they often found at agencies because tickets were in such demand. If *Edward* was the show of the moment, Robert was certainly the man of the hour. He never stopped making speeches and raising money for every charity in sight. He was also rather amused by having two employers — Sherek and Miller and he took to playing one off against the other, creating the kind of school-boy fun he had never experienced as a child.

John Huston arrived from Hollywood and tried to get Robert to agree to play Nero in *Quo Vadis,* but he thought the part wasn't really for him — Nero was a rather unsympathetic character.

The February weather in New York was delightful — there was an early spring, and Robert found time to walk in the park with the children despite the fact that he was playing seven performances a week, rehearsing with Jean Arthur for another Lux Playhouse, re-rehearsing the last scene of *Oscar Wilde* for a charity performance, writing book reviews for the *New York Times* and working on his autobiography. And he kept up the social whirl. Ivor Novello, Zena Dare, Gracie Fields, Freddie Lonsdale, Cedric Hardwicke and Mrs Randolph Hearst were just some of the people he dined with that month, as well as giving a children's party for St Valentine's Day.

Robert was also busily arranging an Australian tour.

124

Gilbert Miller planned to keep *Edward* on after Robert left and had a good deal of trouble finding a replacement. A film name, they decided would be best to keep the play going through the hot New York summer when the city was full of visitors from out of town. George Sanders was the first choice, but that fell through when he married Zsa-Zsa Gabor. Eventually they settled on Dennis King, an English actor who had lived in America most of his life.

The J. C. Williamson Organization run by the Tait Brothers was going to manage the tour of *Edward* in Australasia. They were well known for intimidating English actors, most of whom returned from Australia absolutely hating the whole experience. Robert decided if there was to be any intimidation he was going to do it himself. John Tait, who was nearly eighty, arrived from Melbourne to see the show and settle the contracts. Henry Sherek reserved two good seats for him, but Robert vetoed them. After all, they were playing every night to standing room. Tait wouldn't get the proper atmosphere seated comfortably in the stalls. He was allowed to stand at the back looking at the stage over a row of heads. After the show Robert took him to the grandest and noisiest night club in town, the Copacabana, where over the drumming and general hubbub he got him to agree to the most favourable terms — from Robert's point of view.

By mid-April they were packing up. But before leaving New York MGM arranged a private showing of the film of *Edward, My Son*. Robert thought it was terrible. Spencer Tracy he thought sulky and boring in the part, and the direction was archaic. Then he reflected that maybe he was prejudiced. But on release the critics generally agreed with him. Only Deborah Kerr, playing the drunken Evelyn, came out of it with honours and her first Academy Award nomination.

Dennis King took over the part of Arnold Holt, and Robert flew back to England, though the plane stopped for three hours in Bermuda with engine trouble and then landed in the Azores before finally making it to London. Joan and Nancy had taken the children back to California.

In their absence building had been going on at Fairmans. There was to be a new sitting-room, a larger kitchen and a new bedroom. Robert was pleased to find the new brickwork ten bricks high when he arrived. And the garden was in full blossom. He visited all the family and friends and found that Joan had been sending food parcels to everyone. A good deal of time was taken up choosing a new sink for the kitchen, tiles for the bathroom and trying to organize an electricity supply for the house. There was no mains electricity and they had had to rely on a rather ancient and quirky generator for lighting — often being plunged into darkness just as they were bathing the children. There was also the question of where the chimney should go. Decisions had to be made quickly as Robert was due back in New York for a television broadcast of *Edward, My Son*. But he found time to buy his first race horse, a bay yearling colt by Umidad out of Boston Stump. Robert decided to call it the Gloomy Sentry from a line in *Edward, My Son*.

A private detective called Prothero is watching the flat of Holt's mistress, Miss Perry, and Holt realizes that he can't continue the liaison.

Arnold: I don't know how to say good-bye.

Miss Perry: Don't you? Do you think Prothero is still there? (*Going to the window and looking out*) Yes, still at it. Getting very wet. The gloomy sentry. But I suppose in a way he's the winner, you know. Let's give him three cheers.

Sewell joined Robert for his birthday dinner at the Caprice and brought him a cuttings book for the horse. They hoped to fill it with newspaper stories when he became a winner.

After one last conference about the house Robert set off for New York again. The plane got within three hundred miles of Gander, where it was to refuel, and found the airport fogbound so it turned around and landed at Shannon because it was too big to land anywhere else except New York. He very nearly hired a private plane at great expense to go back to London but instead hired a car to drive the hundred miles to Galway to the races. A cable arrived from

126

the New York television producer: 'Start swimming you rat.'
Finally another plane took him to New York via the Azores
and Boston. It was a very long and tiring flight and when he
finally arrived Robert felt quite sick. He was cheered up
however by the news that he didn't have to do the television
show after all. MGM had always objected to the live
broadcast of *Edward, My Son* sponsored by the Ford Motor
Company, because they felt that if everyone saw it on
television they wouldn't come to their film. But there was no
way they could stop it — no way, that is, until finally Louis
B. Mayer rang up Henry Ford. From the very top came the
word that the show was cancelled, although everyone was
paid. So instead of performing in front of the cameras they all
had a day at the races. Then Robert was able to fly out to
California. He had missed the family terribly and was
delighted to arrive in time for Annabel's third birthday
party.

Back by the pool and lazing in the sun with trips to
Yosimite National Park and Reno, Nevada, Robert
despaired of getting work done on the play he was trying to
write. The weather was too wonderful. He half decided to
buy a little house by the sea and become a novelist — though
he found the rich people in California dull. Although from
childhood he had taken after his father in preferring the very
best suite in a hotel, the most comfortable way of travelling,
and haute cuisine, he believed very firmly in working to
attain these pleasures. He never believed, as did his mother,
sister, and all his aunts, that money was a privilege bestowed
by a caring God on people who deserved it, and that it was to
be conserved. Robert always felt it was the most disposable
object in the world. Even people who had earned their
fortunes and then spent all their time and effort thinking up
ways of keeping it in the bank, Robert found tedious. Money
should be spread around. His main amusement at grand
luncheon parties was to shock people by preaching
socialism. But the sun made up for any disappointment he
felt in local politics. The children had both learned to swim
very well, Sheridan had taken to riding, and Joan loved the

127

climate too — perhaps this was the place to live — it was certainly a prospect to consider. They had no desire to move, but there was work to be done in Australia. Gladys decided to go to Honolulu with them and holiday there as she had finished work on *The Secret Garden*.

They arrived in Honolulu on the Pan American Clipper and were met by Elroy Fulmer, who had been at RADA with Robert and was then the director of the Honolulu Community Theatre. They became the centre of social activity on the island for a week. Hawaii was heaven — hot, sunny and rain at night that kept everything green and so encouraged the lush flowers that greeted them everywhere. The Morleys had an apartment at the Coral Strand Hotel on the beach at Waikiki and at the foot of Diamond Head. Robert sat on the verandah and watched the surfers catching the waves. He was fascinated, and couldn't believe it was difficult. Gathering his rubber lilo he waded out to have a go and was washed out before he even started. When he made it back to the sand he found Annabel in tears. She was inconsolable. Robert tried to tell her that it was all right — he would buy another lilo.

'I'm not crying about that,' she finally told him in between sobs. 'Everybody's laughing at you.'

Robert tried to explain that he found it very profitable to make people laugh — but she still couldn't bear to have them laughing at her father.

Robert was less enchanted by an authentic Hawaiian feast, or luau. He decided Hawaiian food was filthy and consisted of scraps of old pig and a sort of gloomy porridge into which everything was dipped, preferably by hand. He declared the food the reason why the Hawaiians were rapidly becoming extinct. However, he did enjoy riding the waves in catamarans.

Robert joining Yul Brynner and Anne Jackson on The Journey

Robert with Wilton in Oscar Wilde

Dancing with Cliff Richard in The Young Ones

The Duke of Marlborough in Cromwell

CHAPTER NINE

GLADYS STAYED BEHIND IN HONOLULU. She had to return to California where she was under contract to MGM. But another member had joined the *ménage*. Morton Gottlieb had sailed from Vancouver to Hawaii to make the trip to Australia as Robert's business manager. They had met in New York, where Morton was Gilbert Miller's general manager. Morton was a theatre addict. He had been Gertrude Lawrence's press agent and also the manager of the Cape Playhouse where he dealt with a succession of stars. Gilbert had decided he needed someone like Mort to help him deal with Robert, not quite knowing what to expect, and then got rather cross when they got on too well together. But Mort looked on Robert not only as a big star but as a member of a family he knew very well. He had known Gladys and indeed dated Joan's half-sister Sally.

When they first met Mort told Robert how much he had enjoyed his performance as Oscar Wilde ten years before, although in fact he had never seen it. It seemed politic to get off on the right foot and Robert never discovered the truth, although he did catch him out on another pretence. Each evening at the Martin Beck Theatre Robert liked to know who was in the audience. He was rather pleased by the succession of famous names who came to see *Edward*. But occasionally there was no one of note out in front so Mort would go to the dressing-room with a few inventions. Until one night he mentioned someone who Robert knew for a fact had died a year before. The enterprise of this manoeuvre rather amused Robert, and besides he liked Mort.

Robert could envisage trouble ahead in Australia with the Williamson Organization and he thought he'd better have someone on his side. Who better than Mort Gottlieb? He asked him to go along as his personal manager. At first Mort refused: How could he leave Broadway? But Gilbert Miller convinced him that he would be a fool to pass up the chance to go around the world and get paid for it.

The RMMS *Aorangi* was a ship of the Canadian Australasian Line - very old and uncomfortable. When they boarded at Honolulu they found the cot which had been supplied for Annabel was much too small. Getting no satisfaction from the steward, Joan sent for the captain, and while he was there she pointed out the general dustiness of the cabin. It was cleaned and a camp bed was supplied, and Robert couldn't have been more impressed by Joan's handling of the situation. He wouldn't have dreamed of summoning the captain.

The journey was slow and tedious. The turbines weren't strong enough to run the electricity, fans, and air conditioning as well as the engines, so they either went very slowly and had cool air or a bit faster and sweltered. There was a tank on the top deck for a swimming pool and that amused the children. Robert spent most of the time dictating short stories about the Hawaiian islands to Mort, *à la* Somerset Maugham.

It was a cool spring when they arrived in Sydney. They were met at the airport by a barrage of photographers, lights and interviewers, and their first few days were totally filled with receptions and broadcasts, but they managed to find a charming house with a garden and a private beach right on the harbour at Point Piper. Robert found Australian theatrical procedure not so much old-fashioned as non-existent. Tickets were not sold at the box office in the usual way. In fact the box office wasn't opened until seven o'clock, and then only to sell tickets for that evening's performance. During the day, tickets were sold at music shops or book

130

stores but only for that week — as Robert pointed out to them 'Why would anyone go to the butcher's shop for a loaf of bread?' If anyone wanted to book ahead it was necessary to write in and pay extra for the privilege. This, Robert pointed out, was no way to fill a theatre. Moreover he felt strongly that Williamsons's weren't publicizing the show properly. Here they had a show that was a major hit in both London and New York, and they weren't telling anyone about it. Although he generated a good deal of personal publicity, he kept meeting people who didn't actually know why he was in Sydney or, if they had heard about *Edward,* they had no idea where it was playing or for how long. Also, penny-pinching managements had always annoyed him, and if Williamson's could cut corners, they did. Robert insisted on proper props rather than the papier mâché type he was offered. During rehearsals he took to ordering morning coffee and afternoon tea for the cast and charging it to the management. 'Just as well he's not playing the lead in *Annie Get Your Gun,*' the Williamson's representative commented rather sourly.

The first night didn't go as smoothly as Robert thought it should, with a good deal of delay with scene changes. However, no one else noticed — and the party Robert gave at Point Piper after the show was a triumph. Sydney hadn't seen anything like it for years. Joan organized turkey dinner and meringues for more than a hundred guests. Robert hired a pianist, and Mort put on a firework display at one o'clock in the morning. The neighbours were rather amazed but most of them put on dressing gowns and slippers and came out to watch.

Soon after the opening night a young man named Michael Blakemore turned up in Robert's dressing-room. He was an unwilling medical student, rather pressed into it by his father who, a doctor himself, frowned on his son's theatrical ambitions. But Sydney society was a small circle and Michael met Mort at a party one night. Mort mentioned that Robert was displeased with the publicity — or rather the lack of publicity — being offered him and that he was displeased with Williamson's in general. Michael suggested that he do an interview with Robert for the university paper, which would be good publicity among the students, so Mort arranged a meeting between the matinee and evening shows on Thursday. But Michael had ulterior motives. He didn't dare reveal them in the dressing-room with Mort there. After all, Robert's manager was supposed to protect him from intrusion, not introduce it. Michael did his interview and drew a sketch which Robert suggested he finish in the car as he had promised to see the children before they went to bed. They all piled into the car with Robert at the wheel. Mort got out at Kings Cross, where he was staying. At last Michael found himself alone with Robert. He took a deep breath — it was now or never.

'Mr Morley,' he said, 'I've got a few ideas for publicity.'

Robert looked at him rather ruefully and didn't say anything. Michael chattered on and still Robert said nothing. They got to Michael's destination, Robert stopped the car and, leaning across, silently opened the door for him.

'I've just got a few more ideas, Mr Morley,' he said, making them up frantically. He had to speak quickly before he lost his courage. 'Could we drive on to your house and I'll get the tram back?' He'd never get such an opportunity again. Robert closed the door — still saying nothing — and drove on for another ten minutes while Michael talked as persuasively as he could. Finally the car came to a halt, and Robert turned to the young man.

'So you want a job?'

'Well, no — I mean — I've just got these ideas,' Michael spluttered, 'and really I would like to try them out. And I'm willing to work for nothing.'

'My boy,' Robert said, 'never do anything for nothing. Ring me in the morning.'

And so Michael Blakemore got his first job in the theatre — well, connected with the theatre. Robert paid him £3 a week and Robert's co-star, Sophie Stewart, paid him another £3. He was to be their private press representative. For his first assignment Michael was told by Robert to go behind the set and copy down all the previous productions

132

for which the flats had been used. The names of the shows were stamped on the back. Williamson employees watched him suspiciously. Some of the flats went back to a production of *Maid of the Mountains* done in 1922. Evidence of parsimony would be a weapon in Robert's arsenal if the battle turned from a cold to a hot war.

Robert enjoyed the city of Sydney in a limited way. The climate was good and the house perfect, but he sometimes despaired of the Australians he met. They seemed to be interested in nothing more than a day out at the beach, and lots of rather badly cooked meat. And he often shocked them — sometimes purposely, but just as often not. He didn't fit into the pattern they expected of him. It was true that he spoke 'posh' and that he dressed in the Savile Row manner - these and the facts that he was intelligent and English should have added up to a true blue Tory gentleman. Yet Robert preached socialism at dinner parties and told the newspapers when opening an art gallery that he thought all paintings should be done in gradually disappearing paint so patrons would have to buy new ones every so often as the old ones faded, thus giving lots of work to artists. Revolutionary talk on the one hand; facetiousness on the other — it was not at all what they expected. They also found it difficult to comprehend his whirlwind activity. If he wasn't at the theatre or the races or taking the children to the zoo he was opening charity fêtes, broadcasting plays on the Lux Radio Theatre, writing, organizing an outing or having his picture taken packing food parcels for Britain. This was not the life of a country squire.

His sense of humour was sometimes over Australian heads, too. One simple domestic joke in the newspapers caused a furore. Sheridan had spent a term at Cranbrook school, and was about to compete in their sports day. When he asked Robert what he would give him if he won the gold cup for the best all-round performance, Robert thought for a moment. Sheridan nudged him on. Other boys' fathers had promised them prizes ranging from money to a new bike. 'My son,' Robert told him, 'I shall give you Sydney Harbour

Bridge.' This was a very safe promise considering Sheridan's physique (which echoed Robert's) and his unathletic temperament. The citizens of Sydney were not pleased. How dare he regard their greatest pride with such flippancy? Letters poured in rebuking him. Robert also made the mistake of calling Sydney 'a honky-tonk town with a lovely harbour', in front of the press. On the same occasion he also criticized the trams, the fact that too many theatrical stars were imported and not enough were home grown, that there were too few theatres and no open air cafes, that Australians were too keen on ordering people about, and that there were disgraceful drinking laws which closed the bars at 6 pm. At the same time as they were writing 'How dare he?' letters to the papers, the locals were turning up every time he opened a fête or gave a lecture. Six hundred people arrived for a lecture on the theatre which Robert gave at the Mitchell Library; three women fainted in the mob, and others suffered minor injuries as they pushed and jostled to get into the lecture room.

Edward, My Son closed in Sydney at the end of November. All the fussing with 'The Firm', as the Australians called J. C. Williamson's Organization, had paid off, with record attendances for a dramatic show in that city.

The next stop was Melbourne, and the *ménage* increased. As well as the children, Nancy and Mort, the daily they had acquired in Sydney went with them, and Michael Blakemore was sent ahead to prepare the way. His salary increased to £10 a week. No one had seen the house they were going to rent in Melbourne because Joan was ill for three weeks with jaundice and hadn't been able to fly there to reconnoitre. Michael was given strict instructions that there be no press to meet them at the airport. Robert wanted to get the family settled in before beginning the publicity circus. Michael went to all the Melbourne newspapers and begged them not to come. He promised that Robert would give a press conference the day after he arrived. Reluctantly they agreed. Rather pleased with himself, Michael met the family at the airport and drove to the house. It was not as nice as Sydney but adequate, though sparse on furniture. Robert was just congratulating him on his work, and they had barely sat down to tea when a reporter who had climbed over the garden wall appeared at the window and begged for 'Just one picture — *please*, Mr Morley.' The next day a jolly photograph of the family around the tea table appeared in the *Sun,* scooping all the other newspapers, and there in between Annabel and Sheridan, grinning broadly, was the man who had personally begged the editors for no publicity. Michael's credibility as a press agent vanished and he was put to work tutoring Sheridan, who wouldn't be in Melbourne long enough to go to school there.

Robert found Melbourne rather provincial after the semi-sophistication of Sydney and her citizens a good deal more touchy. There were, of course, still the races, and he was in the money so far for the Australian season. However, he lost most of it to the editor of the *Sydney Herald* in a bet on the election. In New York he had met Robert Menzies who had assured him that he would be the Australian Prime Minister when Robert was there, but Robert hadn't believed the Australians would ditch Labour. Still, after the event Robert didn't think a Liberal Prime Minister could do much with a Senate that remained Labour. Robert's politics have always been more visceral than intellectual.

Although Robert had never been very fond of strange dogs — in fact since childhood he was rather terrified of them — he couldn't accept the generally careless attitude of the Australians to their pets. One night on the way to the theatre he saw three boys abandoning a puppy by the roadside. He stopped the car and popped the little dog in with him. After the performance that night he brought it out on stage. 'Would anyone in the audience like to adopt Edwina?' he asked. Dr and Mrs Fabingi volunteered and took Edwina home to Toorak, where they already had four children and two cats. All nicely settled, Robert thought, except that two members of the audience were heard in the foyer on their way out muttering that the play was a lot of nonsense about a dog.

Robert thought that Melbourne was better laid out than Sydney, with wide streets and a great many parks and squares, but found the shopping centre and most of the buildings very ugly, and the general attitude very Victorian. And he never hesitated to say so when journalists asked the inevitable 'What do you think of our city, Mr Morley?'

One day he decided to take a closer look at the Australian drinking customs which he had been complaining about since his arrival. Michael Blakemore took him off with some of his university friends — all serious drinkers. The pubs closed at six, which meant that people stopping work at five or half past would fit in an evening's drinking in under an hour. Robert sat there watching, totally silent for a change, while all around him people swigged their drinks back as if in a competition. The bell rang and he and Michael walked to the theatre along the streets of Melbourne as the pubs were disgorging their patrons. There was a good deal of reeling about and vomiting in the gutters. Unfortunately there was a journalist waiting at the theatre for him that night and next morning the headlines blazed: 'Morley describes Melbourne as a city of Hogarthian Squalor.' That, added to all the other criticism, did not please the inhabitants of Melbourne. But they remained fascinated to see what he would do next and duly reported a Christmas family barbecue, and a photographer was sent along to watch a prospect for gold that Robert organized. The theatre company and the Morley family were photographed panning for gold and finding only minute specks of gold dust.

Despite this keen interest in everything Robert said and did, the natives began to hit back at his criticisms. 'He told us what was wrong,' one columnist reported, 'rather boorishly, exhibiting none of the mature dignity in which he had found us such short-comers. And like so many of our overseas critics, he waited until he got the last penny he was likely to get before speaking up like such a brave wee man. He tossed his cap into the ring and then headed out of town like streak lightning.' The controversy over whether he was right in his criticisms or indeed should even have the audacity to voice

136

them, raged in the press. 'Are we too thin-skinned?' reasonable voices asked. Robert was delighted by all the fuss he had stirred up. Nothing like a bit of excitement to brighten a dull day — or a city, for that matter.

The travelling troupe was soon off to New Zealand, leaving the argument to continue without them. And also leaving Michael Blakemore behind. He was due back at university to continue his medical studies, and was desolate. Anything in the theatre would be better than that.

'Well, Michael,' Robert said to him one day, 'what are we going to do with you? Do you want to be a publicist all your life?'

'I think — what I mean is — ' Michael hardly dared say it, but he had learned over the months that one thing Robert couldn't abide was shyness. It wasted so much time. Say what you think, was his motto — and if you don't think something, say anything. You could always change your mind later. 'I'd really like to be a director.'

'Well, you'll have to develop a great deal more personality than you've got at the moment.' That remark was to haunt Michael for the next fifteen years. But Robert continued, 'I think you ought to be an actor. Actors can get away with anything, you must do an audition for me.'

Michael, being a very innocent twenty-one-year old, thought it a wonderful idea. He found a drama coach in Melbourne and rehearsed the part of Edmund in *King Lear*. An actor in the company agreed to play Gloucester for him. One night after the show Michael put on his best blue suit, made up with Leichner five and nine and put lots of black lines round his eyes. He felt very professional. The stage manager left the stage lit and Robert assembled the company in the stalls. Michael strode on stage and swallowed hard. Then he did his scene.

He was in a state of shock afterwards. The company had applauded politely but he was pale, shivering and silent when Robert took him out for a meal.

'You weren't very good,' Robert began and all Michael's hopes crashed. 'But', Robert continued, 'you did do something which most young actors don't do — you stood stock still the entire time. That's a good thing to do. I think you should go to England and study at RADA. I know Sir Kenneth Barnes very well. We'll write you a letter and see if we can't get you in.' Robert also knew about his family situation and that his father would object strongly. It was a situation he was familiar with. Hadn't his own family rather objected when he went on the stage? Wasn't his mother still disapproving? 'I'll write a letter to your father, too, and tell him it would be the best thing for you to do.' Robert did write to his father, and the letter ended: 'Don't worry about your son. When he's in England I shall keep an eye on him — possibly the blind one.'

That matter settled, the Morleys packed up their seventeen pieces of luggage and sailed on February 13th on the *Dominion Monarch* for Wellington, New Zealand. What they didn't know was that John Tait from 'The Firm' had written to the New Zealand tour director of *Edward, My Son*: 'Morley is a very difficult man, finds fault with almost everyone from the Taits and the organization onwards. He can even be rude to the man in the street, as it were. He is an outstanding actor and it is an equally outstanding play, and it is hoped he will keep to what he is engaged for. Morley has been so antagonistic to the stage manager, Alan Chapman, who happens to be a talker, that he had begged us to relieve him in favour of the assistant stage manager, Tony Ward, who can cope with temperamental artists and who doesn't get on Morley's nerves.'

Wellington was delightful. Robert found it a relief not to see drunks in the street. It was quiet, sunny and warm. The Hotel St George was extremely comfortable, though the delicious suet puddings played havoc with the diet that both Robert and Sheridan had once again embarked upon. Sheridan had inherited his father's love of good food, and both were forever trying to lose weight, promising themselves they would indulge in puddings only once a day — though neither of them kept to it. Robert and Joan spent their tenth wedding anniversary driving around the

138

countryside in a huge American car which they had been lent. Business in the cosy little theatre was fairly good and the audiences extremely receptive. Robert gave his ritual lecture to the amateur dramatic society, and meekly submitted to being shown the view from the top of the Riviera-like hills about six times by various hosts.

He was pleased that the children had adapted to hotel life so well — on the whole they had weathered the years on the road remarkably. But he was beginning to realize how expensive it had been to take the family on the tour. He was once more toying with the idea of giving up acting for a while and writing a book, but he didn't see how he could afford it. 'The trouble,' he wrote to his mother, 'with earning a huge income which is all taxed is that you have to keep earning enormous sums doing films and things which you don't want to do particularly. I think it would be better to restrict my income in the future which may of course mean restricting my expenditure a bit too!' But he didn't mean to begin right away. In Christchurch, at the United Service Hotel, they lived in the suite that had been built for the Duke of Windsor. Christchurch was a very elegant little town with beautiful parks and a little river. The snow-capped Southern Alps glistened in the distance. The people were nice, but the theatre wasn't full.

The flight from Christchurch to Auckland was very rough. They flew very low over the sea to avoid the storms and arrived a quarter of an hour late, which wouldn't have mattered except that they had an invitation from the Governor-General to dine at Government House. They had even been invited to stay there, and Robert relished the idea of writing to his mother on the headed stationery — that would have impressed her at last — but the dates just didn't fit in with the tour. They would have made the dinner in ample time but the car bringing the luggage from the airport broke down and they had to change for dinner. In the end they were only forty minutes late and enjoyed the whole evening immensely — the Governor-General gossiped about Churchill and Barrie and served foie gras and champagne, and Robert began to wonder if perhaps his mother hadn't been right and he should have become 'something in the Empire'. The quiet elegance of it all was most charming. If he had to live in the South Pacific and it couldn't be Hawaii, Robert decided that New Zealand would suit him nicely. Except, of course, for one major problem. The New Zealanders were not theatre-orientated. They had lost — if indeed they had ever had — the habit of theatre-going. The tour of *Edward* lost money there. Still, he couldn't become as incensed with them as he had with the Australians. They were, he found, a charming, hard-working and hospitable people. He was gentle with his suggestions. And despite the fact that his laundry had been stolen and Sheridan's watch was removed from his bedroom while he slept, he had nothing but praise for New Zealand's hotels. He was most impressed by the five course dinners and the sorbet after the roast and before the game. The hotels were, he told the Rotary Club, 'as good as any he had seen in other parts of the world, America included', unlike Australian hotels which he described as 'absolute hell'. There was, however, a good deal to be desired as far as New Zealand theatre was concerned. And Robert thought the businessmen could do something about it: 'As was done with brilliant success in the English industrial city of York, businessmen could get together and establish a good repertory theatre with advantage to Auckland and endless amusement for themselves. Get a reputable professional producer you can trust, form a board of management, and you will find there is nothing more pleasant than running a theatre. Unbelievably, you will also find that in time you will make money and once established, it will become a source of tremendous pleasure and pride.'

There in sunny Auckland, to less than full houses, Robert was to close *Edward, My Son* that last week in March. It had given him three years of work and pleasure and taken him around the world and he was grateful, but not sorry to see the end of it. At the Saturday matinee that last week he decided to make a slight change. Holt's son Edward had never been seen - nor had his grandchild, Edward's son and namesake.

He remains upstairs unseen as Holt leaves the house. 'All right, Edward, you can come down now, there's a good boy,' Parker calls up the staircase and a large toy balloon bounces down the stairs before the blackout. But for this one performance Sheridan followed the balloon down and said, 'How do you do, Dr Parker.' It delighted Sheridan, and his only regret was that he hadn't been allowed to do it all the time.

So *Edward* was over and it was time to go home. But not in any great rush — there was an expedition to the geysers and sulphur springs first, and then a trip back to Sydney where Robert told the assembled journalists he had been joking and of course he loved Australia. He promised to be back soon. They boarded the P & O liner, *Stratheden*. Robert spent his days gossiping and playing bridge and half wondering what to do next. There had been a cable from Carol Reed offering him a film.

Leaving the children on board to continue on to England with Nancy, Robert and Joan disembarked at Bombay in the middle of the worst heat wave to hit the city for seventy years. The English community wined and dined them and showed them the sights. Only at the Wellington Club did Robert find a mixed Anglo-Indian membership — and all the swimming pools seemed to be for the white settlers. Robert decided that India had been lost to the Empire not so much through bad management as through bad manners. Taking to heart his latest resolution about cutting expenditure, he paid his bill for four nights at the Taj Mahal hotel in Bombay with the promise of two free tickets for any play he ever did. A wise move, he thought, as he figured that to break even the proprietor would have to see him 180 times in London, 90 times in New York and 400 times in India, where he was unlikely to play.

They flew next to Cairo, where Robert rode a camel round the pyramids and managed to beat Joan in a donkey race across the desert. Then they went on to Rome. It was Holy Year and the pilgrims were flocking to the Vatican. Graham Greene was there reporting on it for *Life,* and Peter Brook had flown in, not so much to see the Pope — although with the Morleys he attended a semi-private audience — as to bring to Robert the script of *The Little Hut*. Robert was flattered, and on reading it thought it too good to be true.

From Rome Joan and Robert went on to Naples (having glanced quickly at the ruins of Pompeii which he pronounced boring), and then Capri. They could happily have stayed forever lotus-eating at the Hotel Quisissino. Arriving in Italy after the Australian tour was very like stepping into a hot bath after a long day's travelling. Just to laze on the beach forever — never to give another interview or find another house, or have to fill another theatre.

But it was only a dream. Life had to be got on with — the children would be arriving in London on the 20th. Although Nancy was taking them to stay with Buck in St John's Wood, they couldn't be left there forever. Gladys was opening a new play in London, and besides Robert had decided to be home for his forty-second birthday.

CHAPTER TEN

ROBERT HAD A NEW AGENT. It is generally thought that there is a particular period in people's lives when they make deep and lasting friendships — and for most people that period is somewhere in their twenties, or perhaps earlier. Robert had made friends like that, especially Sewell Stokes, Peter Bull and Ambrosine Phillpotts. Most friendships made after that period are more transitory and, although at times lasting, of a more casual nature. But while in New York playing *Edward, My Son,* Robert had met Robin Fox. Robin was a tall, distinguished-looking and very handsome man. His mother, Hilda Hanbury, had been an actress. Robin had been educated at Harrow and practised as a solicitor. In the war he had achieved the rank of Colonel and been awarded the Military Cross. After the war he joined the Music Corporation of America. He was an artist's agent. But as well as being strikingly attractive, he inspired confidence. No matter what the problem, Robin could handle it. He was also an excellent negotiator. Robert has often spoken of the relationship between an actor and his agent as being a kind of marriage. As he so quickly and wisely chose Joan for his wife, so too, he chose Robin as his agent. There was a rather turbulent divorce from his previous arrangement with Film Rights, but he would have weathered anything to make the vow which turned out to be until death us do part. So with a new friend, confidant and guide he set off on his post-*Edward* career which might so easily have been an anticlimax.

The Little Hut, which Peter Brook had shown Robert in Rome, was a French play, written by André Roussin, which was still running in Paris after a thousand performances. Although this in itself seemed an excellent reason for doing it in London, there were by no means slight problems. Nancy Mitford, who translated and adapted it, explained the problems in a letter to her mother: 'It's a terribly funny play about husband, lover and wife on a desert island — lover gets very low all alone in the little hut while husband and wife sleep in the big one, insists on taking turns. Husband not absolutely delighted but sees the logic, that they have shared her for six years and might as well go on doing so. Then a handsome young negro appears, ties up husband and lover by a trick and indicates that he will only let them go if Susan will go into the hut with him, which she is only too pleased to do as he is very good looking. "Disgusting," I hear you say. And so on — you see the form. It is terribly funny, *I* think, but I never counted on it much as everyone said the Lord Chamberlain wouldn't pass it. Here [Paris] it has run over three years, a wild success. I've skated over the worst indecencies, in fact the reason I was asked to do it was that I'm supposed to be good at making outrageous situations seem all right. Roussin, the author, an utter love, doesn't know a word of English so I've got away with altering it a great deal.'

She was very excited about entering into the theatrical world, which was completely new to her, and thought it would all be great fun. Rather a lark. But she soon found that theatrical gossip, which was the only kind actors seemed to indulge in, bored her. Binkie Beaumont was going to present the play. He invited her to a dinner party to introduce her to the theatrical world. She noted in a letter who was there: 'Noël Coward, who kisses me now, Gladys Cooper, Robert Morley, Athene Seyler and the Kaufmans and a lot of stage hangers-on. It's dreadful how dull they all are but don't say I said. Also Communist I note.'

Peter Brook was to direct. Brook was something of an intellectual and had often been termed a genius.

Shakespeare, Shaw and Sartre had been the authors he most frequently worked on, and he came to *The Little Hut* straight from Stratford where he had directed John Gielgud as Angelo in *Measure for Measure*. Although he had worked on French plays he seemed a strange choice by Tennant's for this light, frothy farce, but Brook had always said he wanted 'to change and develop and dreaded standing still'.

David Tomlinson had been the excellent choice for the lover — an elegant, witty actor making a return to the stage after years in films. But the casting of Susan, the wife, presented more of a problem. It was on that character that the play would pivot, becoming either a dirty joke or a sophisticated amusement. She had to be elegant and desirable but remote. Robert knew just the girl. Before the war he had met her in New York where she played frequently in radio plays. He hadn't seen her for years though, and thought perhaps she had given up acting. 'Joan Tetzel,' he remembered her name out loud.

'She was in my office this morning,' Beaumont said.

Robert decided it was fate and advised Binkie to hire her. Oliver Messel, who had worked with Brook earlier in the year on the Anouilh-Fry *Ring Round The Moon,* designed the fairy-tale sets and Balmain was very expensively brought in to design a dress for Joan.

Robert enjoyed *The Little Hut* enormously. Rehearsals were lively because he and Peter Brook did not get on. To direct Robert at all requires great subtlety and the knack of appearing not to direct at all. But Brook had ideas. He believed the director of a French comedy in England should intensify any foreign element for the benefit of English play-goers. He wanted to deal with concepts but found that essentially in *The Little Hut* his painstaking work was largely a matter of the technical timing of jokes. Robert decided Brook enjoyed rehearsals for the sake of rehearsing; he himself had always hated them as being too much like school.

Joan and the children travelled north with Robert and while he rehearsed in Edinburgh, the children played on the

145

sands at North Berwick. The Edinburgh audiences, according to Nancy Mitford, 'screamed with laughter throughout and clapped and cheered for ten minutes at the end.' She was delighted, surprised and encouraged. Before the first night she had expected the worst. 'I'm so ground down by physical miseries I can think of 0 else. Tired (went from the train at 8 to rehearsal till past 2) and hungry . . . Then I'm low about the play. The girl is simply awful. I thought so when I came for rehearsals but they all said she'd wake up, which in my view she hasn't. However, she's quite lovely looking which is a help. Morley is blissful. But I rather dread tonight.' However, after the relief of the first night when the play was 'an absolute whizz' and finding the notices encouraging — 'even the old *Scotsman* is on its side', she discovered the realities of play-writing. 'Now,' she reported, 'there is a lot of work to be done on it . . . Certain bits fall very flat. I sit with script, and note which ones, and next day I rewrite them. Then see how that goes and so on . . . It is a *most* laborious and I see *most* necessary process.'

Robert, as usual got a cold during the tour.

The Little Hut opened at the Lyric Theatre on Wednesday, August 23rd, and the reviews were mixed — but good box office. Roderick Mann thought it 'absurd and delightful. It is also one of the gayest things in London's theatreland.' J. W. Lambert reported: 'Mr Robert Morley, alternately padding and tittupping about the scene, presents a husband volcanic in astonishment, palsied in dismay, and copious in rediscovered joy; here is brimming abundance, quick with mischief and delight.' But David Lewin began a criticism of Robert that would follow him for years to come. He ended his review in the *Daily Express:* 'What a pity about Mr Morley. His talent should never have been wasted on a bedroom farce dressed up for the tropics.' The *Sunday Chronicle* was incensed. 'In the third act immorality is capped by snobbishness and the curtain falls on downright vulgarity.' John Gay 'was embarrassed and so were many people around me. Maybe the censor needs a new pair of glasses.' They were indeed effective reviews and the Lyric

Theatre was to be filled for more than two years.

The vulgarity on which the curtain fell was a monkey half-way up a palm tree. Usually the monkey suit was filled by William Chappell. But sometimes during the run he couldn't appear. Then it was donned by the assistant stage manager, a girl called Rosalind Chatto. She had worked for Tennant's as an ASM ever since they had discovered in one show her ability to cook a perfect omelette in the wings and hand it over surreptitiously to Gertrude Lawrence, who presented it on stage as her own. Robert also discovered her culinary talents and had her cooking elaborate meals for the company between the matinee and evening shows on Saturdays. It was the first of her many talents he was to discover.

The Little Hut was a smash hit. Now settled into the Lyric, Robert found himself involved in a variety of activities in his spare time. The building at Fairmans was finished. He was helping Joan choose carpets and curtains. Mitzi, the pekinese who had been with them since their marriage, had developed heart trouble and he had to take her to the vet to be put to sleep as Joan was too upset. Mornings were often spent supervising Annabel's breakfast, which could drag on for hours, while Joan took Sheridan to day school in Henley. Sheridan's schooling became a major preoccupation. He was coming up to ten and it was high time he went to a proper school. Although, remembering his own hatred of schooldays, Robert was loath to send him away to boarding school, Wargrave in 1950 wasn't full of satisfactory day schools for boys. Robert put an ad in *The Times:* 'Apprehensive parent with gruesome recollections of his own schooling would like to know of one where his son would be really happy and learn to think for himself.' He got plenty of crank replies, but there was one which seemed possible, and Robert went to investigate. 'Sizewell Hall is a large mansion once owned by the Ogilvies where Lady Bull [Peter's mother] who lunched with us last week told me she stayed. The house has its own private beach of a mile and really wonderful grounds,' he reported to his mother, no doubt emphasizing the care he was taking with his son. He wasn't

147

just going to send him off to any fashionable school. 'There are only 37 children, boys and girls, and a very young staff headed by a Dutchman whom I liked on sight, and who like me doesn't think much of cricket and endless hours spent in organized games. He does keep the children well fed and it's the only school I struck where they can have second helpings of everything at all the meals and where they produce their own magazine without a mention of second elevens etc. and seem to preserve their individuality and sense of humour and to be really friendly with the staff. There seems to be an atmosphere of tolerance about the whole place.'

Sheridan had a look at it, too, liked it, and was placed in the care of Harry Tuyn, the extraordinary Dutchman who would remain an important influence in his life for many years.

That settled, Robert spent most days working on *The Full Treatment,* a play he was writing with Wendy Hiller's husband, Ronald Gow, for Gladys.

After Christmas he was occupied once more with filming. *Outcast of the Islands,* based on a story by Joseph Conrad, was being directed by Carol Reed, a man Robert felt happy to be working with as he was so pleasant. He was also cheered by the fact that Wendy Hiller was playing his wife, since he found her fun on the set. His only problem was that they might expect him to help with the script and he found it difficult to know what Conrad was driving at most of the time. Annabel, now four and a half, had graciously consented to play his daughter in the film on the understanding that she would be allowed to have false plaits. Robert thought she was very good at acting but decided that one film was quite enough for her as it didn't take her long to begin fussing about her make-up.

The first Sunday in February there was a charity performance at Drury Lane and Robert decided to resurrect the last scene from *Oscar Wilde* once again as he thought it a good party piece. Although the filming was going pleasantly it was slow. Robert had long conversations with Ralph Richardson (who had married Meriel Forbes-Robertson,

148

his one-time fiancée) about the after-life but they didn't settle anything, to Robert's relief.

Robert hated the fog which closed in that February. He had to be at the studios at eight which, considering the fog, was often a two-hour drive. Then there was *The Little Hut* at night and he never got to see Fairmans in the daylight. He didn't see all that much of it in darkness. The kitchen garden was a quagmire and he was determined to get it properly drained — but there was no time.

The Royal Family came to *The Little Hut*. As the King disliked boxes they sat in the middle of the front row. It was a great boost for business — if the show had needed any. It was the first play the King had attended of his own free will for years, except for the Crazy Gang at the Victoria Palace. The proprietor of the Taj Mahal Hotel also turned up, claiming his first pair of free tickets.

Robert decided the time had come to venture into television. He loved television and kept advising his mother, who never stopped moving from flats to hotels and back again all over Kent, to get a set. Programmes were pretty dull when Robert made his British debut. Some days the races were televised, which was the main reason Robert liked it so much — and there was the odd Giles Cooper play. But on July 19th, 1951 when Robert made his first broadcast, the *Radio Times* schedule wasn't sparkling:

 3.0 *Making Flowers*
 3.20 *Andy Pandy*
 3.40 *Dressmaking*
Then closedown till *Children's Half Hour:*
 5.0 *Science in the Orchestra*
 5.10 *Parent-Craft* — the first of a new fortnightly comedy
   series written by Robert Morley.
Then closedown until 7.30, when there was a second showing of *The Debutante's Father,* and at 9.0 (approx) *The Speedway Test Match* from the Empire Stadium, Wembley. 9.50 gave the viewers a repeat of the previous day's *Newsreel* and at 10.10 (approx) the evening closed with the weather forecast and news, but in sound only.

For obvious reasons there weren't many television reviewers in those early days, but one newspaper reported: 'The new children's hour series *Parent-Craft* looks like being a winner for all ages, if it can keep up the high-spirited standard of yesterday's first instalment . . . This series . . . concerns the adventures of an imaginary family named Pebble — one of those ordinary families of fiction which can become so tedious in less expert hands. There is the usual incompetent father, the harassed but understanding mother, and two bad-mannered children. But Mr Morley has created a living family out of these hackneyed ingredients. The author himself appears in the series as a fussy TV producer looking for a perfect family to feature in a series just like this. Mr Morley enjoys himself hugely in this part and gives himself some delightful opportunities for pulling the BBC's leg.'

Miss Lingstrom, who was in charge of children's television, was persuaded by Robert to allot a special room for the cast and serve a high tea. They started with the cast but Robert encouraged friends, parents and indeed everyone to come, and for the last transmission there were about fifty free-loaders. Miss Lingstrom, when asked to comment on Robert's debut in her field, was reported as saying it was not an experience she would care to repeat.

The summer was sunny and warm. *The Little Hut* continued to pack them in, and for a couple of weeks Robert was filming *The African Queen* with Katharine Hepburn and Humphrey Bogart for John Huston. He did manage to find time to take Lauren Bacall to the races and was amazed that no one except a solitary policeman asked for her autograph.

Joan Tetzel took a month's holiday from the show and Joyce Redman took over during her absence. Sheridan and Annabel went on holiday to Bexhill with Nancy and on August 27th at 6.30 in the morning at Fairmans, Joan gave birth to her third child — a son. They toyed with the idea of calling him Daniel, but in the end decided on Wilton. The first anniversary of *The Little Hut* was celebrated with a party at the Ivy Restaurant and the arrival of Wilton was celebrated with more building plans for Fairmans.

Hollywood seemed still to have Robert classified in the French period mould. This time they offered him *Les Misérables*. He wasn't keen to do it — and moreover he was now in the same position Charles Laughton had been in thirteen years before. He couldn't really afford to go to America, either for a film or to take *The Little Hut* to Broadway.

The African Queen opened in London a few weeks before *Outcast of the Islands*, in January 1952. Robert's part in the former was what could be termed short but showy. He played Katharine Hepburn's missionary brother who dies before the end of the first reel. The *Daily Mail* thought he made 'the most of his few minutes — acting almost with desperation'. The *Sun* thought he was 'superb', and Jympson Harman called Robert's 'a beautiful performance'. Annabel cried inconsolably as she watched him die on the screen.

Outcast of the Islands had been considered for the Royal Film Performance but rejected, possibly, the critics thought, because of the rather exotic native girl, Kerima. Robert had been looking forward to its acceptance so that Annabel could present the customary bouquet to the Royals. When it was released the critics seemed as baffled by the story as Robert had originally been. Roy Nash summed it up, calling it, 'a film rather to admire than to enjoy'. Richard Winnington thought 'Robert Morley's petulant Almayer prodigiously overplayed' and Milton Shulman thought that Robert 'unfettered by script restrictions comes out best with a robust interpretation of the jealous, pompous, grasping Almayer.'

Robert was exhausting an army of tax accountants in the search for solvency. The muddle arose mainly from his years in America and Australia where he had already paid tax on his income. He had come back to England with no profit as it can be very expensive moving a family around the world, and the British tax authorities decided they wanted a great deal of money — based on his gross earnings abroad. Robert just didn't have any money and it looked as though

151

declaration of bankruptcy was the only answer.

'They want £80,000,' he told Joan one night when he returned from one of his endless conferences with accountants.

'Oh,' she said, 'The man laid the wrong lino in the bathroom. I wish you'd take a look at it.'

Robert couldn't believe it. Had she heard him? He repeated the taxman's request.

'Well darling,' Joan said, 'We certainly can't do anything about that. But we can get the lino right.'

Then began the endless round with the taxman which Robert finally accepted as part of a vast existential game. He had to work very hard to earn enough money to pay the tax people, who would then demand tax on that. There was no way of getting ahead of the game. He would have been pleased to come out even, but the accountants pointed out that the only way to do that was to become deceased and that was rather too high a price to pay.

The next film he made, while still playing at the Lyric every night, was *The Story of Gilbert and Sullivan,* an epic Alexander Korda production about the composers of the Savoy Operas. Robert played Gilbert in a large moustache which he took off whenever possible because it tickled inordinately. Sidney Gilliat was directing but Korda himself kept interfering and having the musical numbers reshot. Annabel donned her false plaits once again and joined the extras in a crowd scene one day, but ended up on the cutting-room floor.

Somewhere the previous winter Robert had managed to fit in a film of farce called *Curtain Up.* This was released at the Odeon, Marble Arch, in May. It was based on a stage play (*On Monday Next*) about the trials of a provincial rep company 'which stand up badly to magnification on the screen', one of the critics reported. 'Everybody tries to be screamingly funny. Robert Morley and Margaret Rutherford sometimes succeed.' But the critics in all fairness pointed out: 'The wave of laughter that comes up from the audiences is as solid as a wall, and it would be stupid to ignore it.'

June meant the Ascot race meeting and Robert was determined to attend. He had applied for tickets to the Royal Enclosure but been refused and was barely speaking to his co-star in *The Little Hut,* David Tomlinson, who had managed to get in. Moreover, The Gloomy Sentry was left at the post in his race and finished nearly last.

The Morleys took a family holiday at the Spithead Hotel in Bembridge on the Isle of Wight. Wilton ate a good deal of sand and Robert found himself fairly bored by all the yachting talk among the fashionable set who holidayed there. He always felt that there was room in a boat for a sail or for him but not for both. He even asked the Commodore of the yacht club to stop firing so many guns as it upset the peke. One day Peter Cadbury saw him walking along the sands, his finger held high, testing the direction of the wind.

'At last,' Peter said to him, 'You've succumbed.'

'Nonsense,' Robert replied, 'I'm trying to decide in which direction to launch my kite.'

At the end of September Robert had a gruelling day before the tax commissioners. It was all very technical and Robert, despite his worries, found it extremely dull. He did manage to fit in a farewell lunch with Sheridan, who was on his way back to school. Other men would have been too worried. Mercifully the commissioners accepted the view that he was not liable for tax on his American and Australian earnings as he was not a resident of Britain at the time, despite the fact that he still had Fairmans. The decision didn't mean that Robert had any money — just that he didn't owe quite so much. But the sums they talked of were so immense that to Robert the problem seemed largely academic, and he rather agreed with Joan that there wasn't much he could do about it, so he had better just get on with what he could manage. Still, the money had to keep coming in and that autumn he worked on two films — one about Dame Nellie Melba and the other a cricketing story by Terence Rattigan, directed by Anthony Asquith.

Gladys now had a house in Henley about five miles away from Fairmans, and they all celebrated Christmas there.

153

Robert left *The Little Hut* in January, after two and a half years, and turned to directing. He and Ronald Gow had finally finished their play called *The Full Treatment*. Robert had had Gladys in mind for the part of the rather bizarre interior decorator who nearly ruins a country solicitor's family by remoulding their home into an impossible riviera garden. But Gladys didn't really think that it worked for her. Neither did Ambrosine when Robert gave it to her, but she agreed to do it. Robert decided to direct it himself and Ambrosine immediately smelled disaster. She found he directed as he would play a part himself, and that technique just didn't work. Moreover, rather like a small boy, he became fascinated by the garden furniture he had had specially made in shapes of animals. They opened at the tiny Q Theatre in Hammersmith, but it just didn't work. *The Times* reported: 'The speeches still sparkle as the clever company holds them up to the light; there are a few clever little surprises; but once we have left the first act behind us it is rather like spending the evening in a bus which, happening to have plenty of time, proceeds in a series of hiccups.' Robert thought *The Times* was probably right, as usual, but he found the play great fun to do. He mostly enjoyed organizing the costumes and the furniture, and promptly installed the bamboo animal chairs in the garden at Fairmans.

At the end of February Robert set out for Italy to make a film called *Beat the Devil*. Robin Fox and his wife Angela went with him. There was a good deal of activity but not much filming going on when Robert arrived, although Robin, his ever-aware agent, pointed out that he was on salary as soon as he put in an appearance. Most of the company was assembled. The production unit and the stars — Humphrey Bogart, Jennifer Jones, Gina Lollobrigida and Peter Lorre — had taken over two hotels, where they were joined by John Huston, the director, Truman Capote, the writer, and David Selznick, the producer. Capote was still writing and rewriting the script and spending a good deal of time on the phone talking to his raven, whom he had left in Rome. John

Huston was engaged in all night poker games, and Selznick was trying to organize everything and causing a good deal of disruption.

The Foxes departed after a couple of weeks and Joan brought Sheridan and Annabel out to join Robert. Wilton, who had measles, was left behind in England with Nancy. One day while out driving, Robert asked his lady passenger to tell him if anything was coming before he reversed into a narrow street. 'Nothing,' she said, and Robert smashed firmly into a very expensive Ferrari.

'I asked you to tell me if anything was coming,' he shouted.

'That was there all the time,' his passenger replied quietly.

His failure to notice it was a very costly mistake as the damage was extensive. But before he gave up driving completely he knocked into a good number of trees and post boxes. 'The pillar box wasn't looking where it was going,' he would explain when challenged.

The film continued in fits and starts as the script got rewritten every evening. Robert wasn't quite sure who the character he was playing was supposed to be but decided he was a crook. Anyway, he was being paid enough money to make the waiting around worthwhile. Once again he was planning to take a year off and write a book. Joan eventually took the children back home and Robert spent his days in a little boat pretending to be shipwrecked. One night they didn't get back to shore until ten-thirty. No one had bothered to note which way the boat was heading as long as the sun was in the right position for filming. They ended up off Sicily and it took them four and a half hours to get home. They spent a week marooned on the Pontine marshes in appalling weather, then Huston managed to film a week's location work in one morning after Jennifer Jones had run fully clothed into the sea for no apparent reason except that, like everyone else, she was bored to tears. Huston had his car waiting on the beach and at noon he got into it and drove away — not to be seen again until studio work began in England.

While Robert was in Italy doing location work for *Beat the Devil*, the Rattigan film called *The Final Test* opened. It was about an old cricketer about to play his last test match at the Oval who desperately wants his son's approval and interest in the game, but the boy is more interested in poetry and, while thousands of youths idolize his father, he idolizes a celebrated poet — played by Robert. C. A. Lejeune said: '*The Final Test* strikes one as perfect entertainment of its kind. It does with skill, wit and affection just what it sets out to do: make us laugh, touch our hearts a little, supply words for some of our unformulated thoughts, keeps us for ninety minutes in the most delightful company and sends us home refreshed and happy.' And of Robert's performance: 'Robert Morley tightly bulwarked in a boiler suit, is magnificent as a lionised literary celebrity.'

Robert arrived back from Italy for studio work on *Beat the Devil* and the opening of *The Story of Gilbert and Sullivan*. There was a gala premiere as the film celebrated twenty-one years of Korda films, and a huge supper party on the stage of the Savoy afterwards. The critics thought that as biography, the film went only technicolour deep, but the musical numbers which swamped the action were nice.

Robert also found a letter from his income tax inspector asking him to write to him as little as possible during May as he was changing offices. Robert would really have preferred never to write to him again. That month the BBC did a radio adaptation of *Edward, My Son* in their Saturday Night Theatre. Howard Marion-Crawford played Lord Holt.

By the last week in May London was given over to Coronation fever. The acting community got in early on the 29th with an extra special gala midnight matinee at the London Palladium organized by Noël Coward and called *Stars at Midnight*. It was in aid of the Actors' Orphanage and the Jewish National Fund Charitable Trust. David Niven, dressed as a commissionaire, met people as they arrived and on stage all the stars were there — Laurence Olivier, Edith Evans, John Gielgud, Humphrey Bogart and on ad infinitum — and into the early hours of the morning Robert

156

compered the show, in verse. They raised £19,000.

But the hooha and paraphernalia surrounding the Coronation began to bore Robert — especially all the pictures of the coach the Queen was to ride in. He thought they could surely have got her to Westminster Abbey a bit less laboriously. Henry Sherek had offices overlooking the route of the royal procession and invited the family to a party to watch it all in peace. But it meant getting up very early in the morning and then battling through the chaos in London. Robert bribed the children to stay at home and watch it all on television. As well as the midnight matinee he had a Coronation week engagement at the Albert Hall. He was to attend a ball dressed as the Prince Regent. He had also been asked to play Henry VIII at the Old Vic in celebration, but he could no more face that than he could the procession.

Robert finally finished *Beat the Devil*, still not quite sure what it was all about. He was rather worried that John Huston would want to do *Moby Dick* next and ask him to play the title part. Although threatening, as usual, to take a year off (he thought the public had had quite enough of him), Robert was working on an adaptation of Roussin's French Farce which Robert called *Hippo Dancing* and continued to do so as they all went off on a family holiday to Cornwall. The Foxes had a house nearby and it was a jolly time with days on the beach and visits to the du Mauriers who lived there.

In November Robert and Joan had a holiday in Morocco without the children, and it wasn't just to avoid the opening of *Beat the Devil*. The critics were bemused by it — and they also didn't much like it, which seems amazing as it went on to become a major cult film. They just couldn't categorize it; the day of the thriller parody was still about ten years away.

Robert made all the headlines in December when he did a guest appearance on the television quiz game *What's My Line?* He sat in for Gilbert Harding, who was one of television's few real 'personalities', while Harding was in hospital with bronchial trouble. He had been a bit daunted by the prospect. In one evening on Britain's most popular

157

show he would be seen by more people than in eighteen years in the theatre. The papers rediscovered Robert and called him the 'TV find of the year. He brought a brilliant wit which turned this programme from a knife-edge affair of tension into the enjoyable romp it always should have been.' Newspaper writers and viewers alike clamoured for him to become a regular fixture but Robert thought not — he had plenty of things to be getting on with.

In early January, although fitting in a few days' filming for MGM, Robert began rehearsals for *Hippo Dancing*. He and Robin had spent much of the previous September in Paris trying to find a French actress for the leading role. What they didn't understand at that time was that non-English speakers can often appear to be quite fluent by keeping to a small vocabulary, but a few words and phrases repeated with the right inflexion are not enough to make a successful West End actress. They had come up with a girl named Colette Proust — with a name like that they felt she couldn't fail. Robert took her to see Yvonne Arnaud, of whom he thought Miss Proust could give a good imitation. She denounced Miss Arnaud as a Flemish freak: 'No one,' she told him, 'speaks like that.' Binkie Beaumont came to a rehearsal and was unable to understand a word Miss Proust spoke. 'Send her home,' he told Robert. 'With a solatium?' Robert suggested. 'Well, don't give her a fortune — give her a fiver,' Binkie told one of his aides.

Brenda de Banzie was brought in and Wilfred Hyde-White co-starred. Joan went over to Dublin for the opening night. The *Irish Independent* thought it 'one of the most enjoyable light comedies staged in Dublin for some years', while the *Irish Times* reviewed it a bit more astringently: 'It is slight in its content, superficial in its treatment and unoriginal in its theme — yet the impeccable acting, the perfect timing and the adroit dialogue combine to keep the audience comfortably cosseted from one laugh to the next until the final curtain. It may not be a good play but it is admirably good entertainment.'

But the Dublin week was just the beginning of the tour. At

Blackpool he spent a good deal of time rewriting the third act. Peter Ashmore, who had directed *Edward, My Son,* was back with Robert on *Hippo Dancing,* and Wilfred Hyde-White and Robert might have been made for each other. They were both always eager to hurry off for a day at the races, and usually did. But Robert did not get on well with Brenda de Banzie, who was playing his wife. However, in Edinburgh she had a fall on stage and hurt her leg. The understudy, Zena Howard, took over and kept the part as Miss de Banzie didn't return. If she had, Robert felt she would probably have stolen the play. But he did find her very difficult and his emphasis — to the detriment or otherwise of the play — was on one big happy family.

They played Newcastle, which was handy for the racing and lunch with the Lord Mayor; Oxford, which was handy for Fairmans; Brighton, which was handy for Robin Fox's home; and then Robert got his customary cold. As there wasn't a theatre available in London it was back on the road again to Cardiff, Bournemouth and Golders Green before settling into the Lyric Theatre again which was rapidly becoming a second home for Robert. They opened there on April 7th, 1954. Robert played Harry (Hippo) Osborne, a Golders Green fruiterer who spends his life fussing and fuming over inessentials and discovers that his two sons are hopeless — one wants to be a dress designer and the other is being kept by an Italian princess. But his wife stands up for the boys in the midst of Hippo's tirades and even considers leaving him. It all comes right in the end — one boy marries the princess, the other wins £5,000 in a fashion competition, and Hippo mellows. *The Times* said: 'This is a comedy which triumphs over the disadvantage of having no spinal column and no recognizable nationality.' The *Daily Telegraph and Morning Post* reported: 'A curious play, and not really a very good one . . . All the same I think it will draw the public. The tremendous gusto of Mr Morley's performance, if it does not carry him off by spontaneous combustion early in the run, will be an irresistible attraction.' The *Sunday Express:* 'Rare entertainment by a remarkable personality.' Robert gave

159

everyone in the cast a cigarette case for the first night and they were in for a long run.

Robert's mother had a couple of minor heart attacks in May and besides visiting her he was busy going down to Virginia Water to see his old pastor Canon Elliot, the man who had given him his first stage performance in a Christmas play. The old man was depressed to find himself very miserable and rather abandoned in a nursing home. Although Robert found his mind wandering a good deal he didn't think this a very fitting end to a spectacular preacher. But the old man was past cheering up.

There was a charity matinee in honour of Sybil Thorndike's jubilee year in the theatre and to mark the fiftieth anniversary of the foundation of RADA at Her Majesty's Theatre. The Queen, the Queen Mother and Princess Margaret were there. *The Times* described Robert's contribution: 'The sole contemporary comic note was sounded by the next piece, "All the way to Zeals" described as "a fragment for posterity" by its author Mr Robert Morley. It was a vehicle for Miss Gladys Cooper and the author himself in which improvising together in the roles of their own personalities one recited the Telephone Directory and the other the ABC Railway Guide. Mr Morley's splendid line, "I will do for the Telephone Directory what Emlyn Williams did for Dickens" brought us laughing to the interval.'

The Rainbow Jacket, a racing film from Ealing Studios, was released that month. Robert and Wilfred Hyde-White played owner-stewards, as one of the film critics put it: 'in their own valuable manner', which meant they made up their own dialogue as always, because they found it easier to remember.

In June, *Hippo Dancing* happily along at the Lyric, Robert was asked to introduce Marlene Dietrich at the Café de Paris. Other notable men had been requested to introduce the legendary lady — in fact 36 in all on 36 consecutive nights. For payment they each brought a party to the night club and watched the performance for which the public were

160

Sampling Vincent Price's cuisine in Theatre of Blood

Theatrical conservation activities
with Diana Rigg

Robert 'stopping the show' on Gladys's 80th Birthday, and (right) celebrating in the stalls

A summer lunch at Fairmans

charged three guineas a head. Noël Coward wrote and recited a six-verse poem for his stint; Michael Redgrave composed and sang a song; Donald Wolfit quoted Shakespeare; and Van Johnson was so nervous he had to be helped up the stairs; but Eve Perrick, columnist for the *Daily Express* reported: 'Robert Morley, brightest and best of the bunch, went on so long that Miss D. whispered: "Has he forgotten I'm on the bill as well?"'

That July the family moved down to a beach house at West Wittering. Robert commuted from there to the theatre. Never a family to travel lightly, they had moved everything that seemed remotely movable and that they could possibly want, including the cat who spent three weeks there miserably in a cupboard and refused to come out.

One August Saturday night after the show Robert and Wilfred flew to Deauville where they spent a happy Sunday losing money at the Casino. Robert paused in his throwing franc after franc away only long enough to gaze in wonder at a man who had won a million and a half francs on one turn of the roulette wheel. It was a very rough flight back and they were both sick, which they took to be divine retribution.

In September *Hippo Dancing* celebrated its 200th performance. Princess Margaret had been to see it, which was good publicity. The Royal Film Performance that November was *Beau Brummell* and it caused quite a stir. The *Daily Express* wondered why instead of just boring the Queen with their yearly selection for the charity premiere, this year the organizers had decided to embarass her. 'Fancy,' Leonard Mosely went on to point out, 'giving your patronage and attention to a film show in which you had to watch: 1. One of your ancestors, George III going mad in St George's Chapel, Windsor, and playing a lunatic game of hide and seek along the corridors of the castle; 2. The Prince of Wales bursting into tears because the Prime Minister refuses to let him marry 'the woman I love' [too close a parallel, Mr Mosely thought, to the Queen's uncle Edward VIII] and 3. Scene after scene in which royalty is turned into a farce and the monarchy played for cheap laughs'. And *Time*

Magazine noted: 'Peter Ustinov plays the Prince of Wales and Robert Morley his dotty papa. These two amiable monsters, as shapelessly as two corpulent snails, seem to be engaged in a contest to see who can stick his long-stemmed eyeballs farthest out of his head. Morley, as the Monarch who "talks to trees [and] mixes paint with his feet", is the winner by a cornea.'

Robert insisted that his mad king in *Beau Brummell* was a good part. 'I played it exactly the same way as Louis XVI [in *Marie Antoinette*] but no one noticed. You see, I'd changed my wig.'

He was master of ceremonies at a Christmas party given at the Café de Paris on Sunday, December 12th in aid of the British Cancer Campaign, and spent much of that month searching assiduously for a gypsy caravan. He had decided that was exactly what the children wanted for Christmas. At last he found one — completely fitted with beds and cupboards and mirrors — and drove it in triumph up Crazies Hill on Christmas morning. The children were certainly surprised.

In Kent, his mother had had a fall from which she never really recovered. Robert spent a lot of time with her, but she did not live out the year. Even though Robert rationalized that 82 was a good age to achieve, it was inevitably a blow.

In February Robert bought himself a new race horse — Brief Span, who was very quiet and well behaved and had a passion for barley sugar. He also bought the rights to a thriller called *The Whisper in the Gloom* which he planned to make into a film after writing a script but never did. Wilfred Hyde-White left *Hippo Dancing* but Robert carried on for a few months more as well as playing yet another French King in a film for MGM, *The Adventures of Quentin Durward*.

In November 1955 Robert set sail for New York once more. He was finally to do a live television broadcast of *Edward, My Son* under the sponsorship of the US Steel Corporation. Ann Todd was to play his wife and Gladys Cooper's daughter Sally was his secretary/mistress. However, Ann Todd, taking over Peggy Ashcroft's part, was

162

the only one to take it seriously. At the dress rehearsal Robert sat at a table to deliver the prologue instead of striding on from the wings. The chief lighting engineer looked at him coolly. 'Do you speak in this?' he asked.

Leueen McGrath, who had created the part of Robert's mistress, was married now to the playwright George Kaufman. They gave a party in their apartment after the transmission. 'You were lucky to get away with that one,' Kaufman remarked to Robert. Robert was very resentful.

New York had many more television reviewers than Britain — and they all agreed that *Edward, My Son* was great television, indeed worth every penny of the expense involved in importing the stars. The *New York Times* reported: 'Whatever had to be cut from the original was not unduly missed; the TV version held together as a dramatic entity in its own right and was thoroughly arresting . . . Mr Morley captured all the subtleties and especially on the home screen his interpretation was magnificent for its revelatory insight . . . *Edward, My Son* was one more addition to this season's list of dramas that bespeak TV's growing maturity.' Another review ended: 'Come back again, Mr Morley.'

CHAPTER ELEVEN

ROBERT CAME HOME looking for a new play. Gerald Savoury, who had had an enormous success with *George and Margaret* eighteen years before, had written *A Likely Tale*. In *George and Margaret* the couple never appeared, and he used a similar device in his latest play. The old man whose money everyone wants is upstairs, unseen. Two sisters, a brother and the brother's son wait for their father to dispose of his money, and bicker about which of them should get it. Peter Ashmore was directing it and he wanted Robert to play the two parts — the son and the grandson. It did mean cutting out some of the better scenes in which they confronted each other, but they assured themselves that the novelty of Robert doing the double role more than made up, for these losses. Savoury wasn't so sure about it.

Violet Farebrother played one of the sisters and Margaret Rutherford was perfect casting for the other. She was in a nursing home in Brighton recovering from a nervous breakdown. Robert decided the best place for her was on stage, and removed her from the nursing home. Just as all those years before he had convinced her that she could excel as a comedienne in *Short Story*, he now convinced her that she could do this part. He installed her at Fairmans during rehearsals. Swathed in a billowing cape, she would disappear into the wind on marathon walks, and always went to bed after supper with a huge tray of sandwiches — all of which would be consumed by morning.

164

A Likely Tale opened at the Globe Theatre on March 22, 1956. The critics were as fascinated by Robert's dual role as he had hoped they would be. Robert Wraight explained to his readers: 'At one point he has us gasping by seeming to change all his clothes and his wigs in 10 seconds flat. One moment he is Oswald Petersham, fat and 65. The next he is Oswald's son Jonah, still fat but only 40.' All the critics seemed to think though, that despite the the spectacle of Robert's doubling and Margaret Rutherford's Mirabelle, 'her curls a-quiver and her chin tremulous', the play just wasn't good enough. Kenneth Tynan called it 'neither good theatre nor bad; it is simply irrelevant theatre'. The public liked it very much though. An extract was shown on April 23rd on television and the show could easily have run longer than it did had not Robert gone into rehearsals for *Fanny*.

He had seen *Fanny* when he was in New York and had loved it, so he was absolutely delighted when he was asked to play Panisse, the role created on Broadway by Walter Slezak. He was not at all daunted by the idea of singing and dancing in an American musical — although he not only had no ear for pitch or tone but also no sense of rhythm. He dismissed all that; if Rex Harrison could do it, so could he. Besides, he only had one number and a tiny dance. He fully intended to be a smash hit at Drury Lane. The producer, who was Maria Callas's impresario and more used to working in concert halls than in theatres, only expected it to run for a year — as *My Fair Lady* was then due to come into the Lane. Robert fantasized about Rex's consternation at being delayed for years because of Robert's huge and long-running success. He threw himself into rehearsals for the first time with gusto and delight. He was fascinated by all the activity involved in a massive musical. William Hammerstein was directing and he too was rather overpowered by the massive undertaking and rather lost sight of the dramatic moments. 'Look dear,' Robert was heard to say to him, 'why don't you pop out and have a lovely cup of coffee and we'll sort this dreadful mess out amongst ourselves. This scene, you see, needs acting. Come back when we need a thousand dancers going in the right direction.'

Fanny was based on Pagnol's French film trilogy about old, unattractive Panisse who desperately wants a child. Fanny is expecting a baby but her lover Marius has deserted her for the sea. Panisse marries Fanny and gives her and her child a loving home while Marius's father César, Panisse's oldest friend, also pines for his son's return. It was a charming story in the original and the music by Harold Rome had some really touching moments — but to fill Drury Lane the show got stretched out of all proportion, and eventually the crowds of dancers and acrobats and circus turns swamped the action completely. It opened on November 16th, 1956. The critics didn't care for it at all — although the worst they said about Robert and Ian Wallace, who played his friend César, was that they were too English to be believable as the garlic-soaked Frenchmen.

Once a show of that magnitude was on at the Lane there was no point in closing it. So much money had already been spent that the thousands the management would lose keeping it going seemed insignificant. Despite the reviews, Robert loved performing in *Fanny*, even though in the middle of the Suez crisis the theatre was often freezing cold. He found it glorious having a twenty-five piece orchestra trying to keep up with him while he sang.

In a big company there are bound to be personality conflicts and Robert spent a good deal of time pouring oil on troubled waters. But besides coping with the animosities, he managed to carry on as if the show was the most enormous hit. There was no air of disaster backstage. Suppers were instituted between the shows on Saturdays with Ros Chatto once again doing the cooking. Usually they took on a theme — French, American, Chinese, Scots, Greek meals appeared. Ros did miss one week, though. She gave birth to her second son rather suddenly, though thanks to the loan of Robert's driver the event did take place in the hospital.

But besides the weekly dinners arranged for the principals, Robert never stopped throwing enormous parties for the whole cast — all one needed to do was mention a birthday or an anniversary or the coming of the full moon and Robert would say 'Oh, we'd better have a party then.'

For Christmas he gave everyone a cast iron anchor with 'Fanny, Christmas 1956' engraved on it. The top pulled out and it was a corkscrew, and soon he was up to his tricks on stage. One night he smuggled a real baby into the crib for the Christening party scene. It howled all through Ian Wallace's song. On another occasion he went to Julian Orchard who was Ian's understudy as well as playing a small part, and asked him: 'Can you make an imitation piece of cake?' Julian felt in no position to refuse the star, and obediently set about contriving a piece of cake. He had a large yellow sponge which he carved into shape — measuring it carefully so that it would fit into the stage cake. Then he iced it with make-up removing cream and put a catarrh pastille on the top to pass for a cherry. Robert was delighted with it and put it into position. All evening he was giggling and rubbing his hands in anticipation. At last the moment came and he passed the cake to Ian, who took a mouthful and promptly spluttered. Ian exploded off stage. 'Well, it was rather foolish to eat it, dear,' Robert told him.

The other scene that brought out the worst in Robert was his death scene in a big brass bed, with his loved ones coming in to bid him farewell. This was the moment the critics had found particularly touching. One by one the friends and relatives would arrive to say goodbye to Panisse, and they were often greeted by the squeech-squeech of Robert unscrewing bits of the bed. Sometimes he would hand Julian a long bit of brass and leave him to get it off the stage somehow, or one of Robert's massive hands would clutch the helpless victim and refuse to let go when it was time for his exit.

Early in the morning of December 17th the phone rang at Fairmans. Robert answered it and found on the other end a Mr Bishop calling from Downing Street. Would Mr Morley, he wanted to know, accept, the appointment as Commander of the Order of the British Empire in the New Year's

Honours list? Robert thought it was a joke. But Mr Bishop wrote very formally assuring him that there was no joke, and the investiture was duly held in March in the white and gold State Ballroom at Buckingham Palace. Robert received the CBE along with Cecil Beaton from Queen Elizabeth as Sheridan and Annabel watched.

During the run of *Fanny* Robert was asked to do a cabaret season at the Café de Paris, the small night club where he had introduced Dietrich. His immediate reaction was 'What fun,' and he called Julian Orchard into his dressing-room.

Dreading being asked to supply props for another prank, Julian appeared.

'I've been asked to do the Café de Paris,' Robert told him, 'and I said I would if you would.'

Julian thought he was joking.

'Really,' Robert assured him. 'Will you do it with me?'

Julian never said no to Robert. So they set about rehearsing various sketches. Julian was always in mime. He played a middle-aged European princess, Robert's butler and his son, Edward. To Julian, still very young in the business, it was like marrying into the Royal Family. He was playing in *Fanny* at night and rehearsing with Robert all day, so he found himself lunching at Scott's and being introduced to all the celebrities. Robert was very nervous about the cabaret and there really wasn't any time for a quick trip to the casinos, so the comforting extravagance of shopping was the only answer. He popped into Fortnum's for a pint of perfume for Joan. He had nearly given up buying her jewellery, as she only put it in the bank.

The first night came and after the curtain fell on *Fanny* Robert and Julian hurried on to the Café. It had been suggested that Julian dress in some coat cupboard as there was only one dressing-room, but Robert insisted that they share it — although, banked high as it was with flowers, there wasn't much room. Julian was relieved to see that Robert looked as scared as he himself felt. The orchestra was playing, soon to go into their entrance music, when suddenly Robert's nose began to bleed. He looked rather like a harpooned whale. Julian, whose father was a doctor, tried to remember what to do. Shaking with nerves, he made Robert lie down on the floor, soaked some tissues in the ice in the champagne bucket, and rammed one up Robert's nose.

'Do you think we ought to cancel, dear?' Robert asked hopefully from his position on the floor as the orchestra played *Land of Hope and Glory,* announcing his entrance.

Julian spent the whole performance wondering if Robert would inhale the tissues and die.

Robert never felt that cabaret was one of his triumphs — but society came to see him in good measure and because it was Robert it worked. Cecil Wilson reported: 'He sang (if he will pardon the word) with the benevolent aplomb of a squire letting his hair down at the tenants' Christmas party. Yes, it was *we* who were *his* humble servants. All but one of his eight lyrics — and that was by Kingsley (*Lucky Jim*) Amis — were his own; all written and delivered with the polish of one of our smoothest after-dinner speakers.' He would invite Lady Docker on stage to help him tear up phone books. Sophie Tucker, who had preceded him in cabaret, said he had a good opening and a good close — pity there wasn't anything in the middle beside good humour. But she helped him tear up phone books too.

It was also during the run of *Fanny* that Robert and Robin and Ros decided to go into management. They got themselves offices in Old Burlington Street across from Robert's father-in-law's club, Buck's 'in case they should ever run out of champagne', and installed a couple of sofas and dining table. Robert absolutely forbade desks. The Robin Fox Partnership was formed and they opened for business. Their very first venture was a play Robert had written with Dundas Hamilton, a stockbroker. It was called *Six Months' Grace.* In it, a wife, played by Yvonne Arnaud, swaps roles with her husband. He stays at home, cooking and nagging, and she tries to run his fruit business. The major innovation in the play seemed to be that all the dresses came from Marks and Spencer instead of some couturier designer. John Barber in the *Daily Express* thought: 'The

169

comedy will do. But only just.' W. A. Darlington thought that the authors 'hardly touch on the real theme of the play to any valid effect. They are content with incidental entertainment which is good enough to keep an audience mildly amused but never aspires to achieve any tension at all.'

The next venture of the Partnership was more successful. They were offered the Broadway success *The Tunnel of Love* and cast Ian Carmichael and Barbara Murray in the leads. Robert directed. It opened in December 1957 and ran until *West Side Story* took over Her Majesty's Theatre the following December.

The Partnership, joined by John Clements, had another success the same month with Ben Levy's *The Rape of the Belt*.

On Sunday, January 5th Robert compered the popular television variety show *Sunday Night at the Palladium*. The *Observer* commented succinctly: 'A glimpse of Robert Morley, compering the early stages of *Sunday Night at the Palladium,* suggested a performing elephant, albeit of genius, participating with utmost reluctance in cabaret in a house of ill fame. This is no way to exploit Morley's vast possibilities as a TV personality.' The *Daily Express* said: 'Morley is one of the few entertainers left who add to the asset of personality a depth, a scathing wisdom, an intelligent tongue, and a brain. But last night he was a disappointment. Why? Because he seemed to play down his own brandy fumed humour to the level of the public bar . . . Only now and again did he allow himself the kind of barbed mickey-taking which this show needs . . . It was a shame that his spontaneous wit turned into a spectral sell-out to the mass audience.' But Robert had a contract to do it three more times that month.

In the Spring of 1958 Robert set out for Vienna to film *The Journey,* stopping on the way in Geneva to see Sheridan who was spending a year at the university there before returning to Oxford. Tom Chatto, Ros's husband, was travelling with him and helping him lose some money at the Casinos along the way. He arrived in Vienna and met Yul Brynner who was not only starring in the film but also putting up a good deal of

170

the money for it. Brynner calmly announced at lunch that he was thinking of having his tonsils out, which everyone agreed would rather hold up the filming. In the event he didn't, although the filming was still held up. Robert spent a good deal of the time with a local dentist trying to overcome the language barrier and get an abscessed tooth mended. Everyone in the company seemed homesick except Deborah Kerr, whom Robert thought very like his mother-in-law Gladys in temperament. 'What bliss it is,' she said, 'to have a holiday in a hotel at the Company's expense.'

No one was very pleased with the script. The story had originally been set in China but to take advantage of the topicality of the Hungarian uprising it had been moved, and the transition was proving difficult. The enormous cast had been assembled and just waited, completing perhaps one take a day if they were lucky.

Anne Jackson, Eli Wallach's wife, was particularly anxious about the delays as she was playing a pregnant American lady — which was indeed her true condition, and nature would not wait indefinitely even if a film company could. Robert kept taking her to see *Madame Butterfly* to cheer her up. Yul Brynner wasn't actually filming yet at all, but he kept turning up every day with his camera and taking endless pictures which the company rather suspected he was selling to magazines.

One day, getting off location work early, Robert and David Kossoff drove off over the hills to a bird sanctuary. Robert had developed a peculiar desire to see a large wild turkey that was native to the region. He never found one but saw lots of storks nesting on the roofs of the villages they passed through. Then they came to the Communist frontier and got out of the car to inspect the barbed wire which lay across the road. A soldier in the watch tower on the other side pointed a tommy gun at them. Robert just lowered his head and walked slowly and casually away pretending he hadn't seen him, and trying to look invisible. Luckily he was still alive when Joan and the children arrived for Easter.

The film moved slowly along. Robert thought they seemed

to make up their minds about shots hourly and change them half hourly. But the script was improving. The director, Anatole Litvak, called in his friend Peter Viertel, who had written the screenplay for *The Sun Also Rises* and *The African Queen*. Deborah Kerr's marriage to Tony Bartley was floundering and in Peter Viertel she found a witty and sympathetic companion. The company watched with fascination as the friendship grew — it turned eventually into marriage.

At last the sun came out and Robert donned his thin suit only to find he couldn't get into it. All those afternoons with hot chocolate and apple strudel and cream had taken their toll. He tried a diet again, struggling to eat nothing but cold roast beef, but Robin and Angela had arrived — and there were so many restaurants to show them. It wouldn't be fair to sacrifice their pleasure for his figure. Eventually he found the Danube had brightened from a cold grey to a nearly blue. And the filming was finished as if by magic, too, so Robert bought two cuckoo clocks and came home, to begin work on the film of *The Doctor's Dilemma,* directed by Anthony Asquith. Louis Dubedat, the character who had meant so much to him as an adolescent when played by Esme Percy, was taken on this time by Dirk Bogarde.

Robert decided to work on another Roussin play — *La Femme, Le Mari, et La Mort* which he called *Hook, Line and Sinker*. It was about a wife keen to murder her fisherman husband. Not being in the mood to scrimp, and deciding that Joan Plowright (who was to play his murderous wife) looked a little pale after her serious work at the Royal Court Theatre, the home of new British drama, he decided to rehearse the company at Juan Les Pins. Well, after all, it was a French play — a little local colour couldn't do any harm.

They opened in London at the Piccadilly Theatre on November 19th, 1958. Felix Barker told his readers: 'If you are a Morley fan, you will probably find this to your taste, though you may miss his usual charm and urbanity. These studied, devastating sarcasms seem a little gabbled, the comic expression rather forced. The truth is this isn't an awfully funny play.' Unfortunately it never became another *Little Hut* and ran only four months, during which time he made another film with Anthony Asquith and Dirk Bogarde — *Libel*.

In March *The Journey* was released. John Waterman summed it up most succinctly: 'One day, possibly, the Hungarian revolt of October 1956 will be appropriately commemorated on celluloid. Meanwhile, *The Journey* . . . must serve as a warning to anyone approaching the subject . . . Despite the elaborate physical trappings, Litvak has contrived a Ruritanian romanticism within the proceedings; a joke Hungarian hotel proprietor, massed peasants appearing on cue to sing national songs, the Red Army permanently stamping round to well-rehearsed songs. The script demands lines such as "One always thought of the Hungarians as a bunch of gipsy fiddlers; now they have taught the world a lesson in courage." Even Mr Morley cannot convey such capsuled sentiment with either conviction or authority. But more important than all this is that *The Journey* really exploits the Hungarian rising as an excuse to tell a story about stock characters in a stagey situation.'

The Doctor's Dilemma came out the following month. Generally the critics found it outdated, stagey and wordy — but worthy.

Hurrying up to Edinburgh and donning a kilt — over his bathing trunks, Robert was careful to point out — he worked in the film version of James Thurber's classic short story, *The Catbird Seat*, to be released eventually as *The Battle of the Sexes*.

Robert turned to directing for the Robin Fox Partnership again. This time his stars were John Neville and Dorothy Tutin and again it was a Broadway success he was working on: *Once More With Feeling*. Bernard Levin and *The Times* critic absolutely hated it. Milton Shulman quite liked it and Dick Richards in the *Daily Mirror* loved it. W. A. Darlington thought that 'if Mr Morley himself at an earlier age had been available he would have been just the actor for the conductor, a part which needed flamboyance and vigour,'

173

but he conceded: 'The play ended well and to a roar of applause and I left the theatre feeling that a good many people had liked it, though I could not be of their number. Try it, and see what you think.' The public didn't try it and in September the company vacated the New Theatre.

But for extravagant, expensive and phenomenal theatrical flops it is hard to beat *The Love Doctor,* which ran for sixteen performances at the Piccadilly Theatre in October of 1959. Robin had been out of town when Robert and Ros had brought to their magnificent luncheon table a musical adaptation of *Le Malade Imaginaire.* The authors told them that they had all the backing for what was bound to be a magnificent success. Really the management need only rubber stamp it all. It turned out to be a very expensive rubber stamp which Robert provided after the numbers from the show had been played for his tuneless ear. The wheels began to roll and Robert went off to the Venice Film Festival once more — that year they were showing *The Battle of the Sexes.* On his return he went up to Manchester to have a look at a try-out of *The Love Doctor* and decided it needed a lot of work — which, holing up at the Midland Hotel, he set about. He rewrote, redirected, cajoled, coaxed and wheedled. Then he wisely flew to America before the first night.

'I was fortunate, I fell asleep,' Bernard Levin headed his review; 'Pass me the morphia,' Robert Wraight begged. *The Times* more sedately reported 'All style and no matter.' Robin cabled Robert: WORST NOTICES SINCE PEARL HARBOUR, and the Robin Fox Partnership never really recovered as a management.

In America, Robert starred in an Alfred Hitchcock television special as well as two drama specials. He also found time to visit Las Vegas, which he insisted was just like Blackpool, and at the Hotel Sahara he played dime roulette round the clock. He also managed a trip with Gladys, who was packing up her California house to return to England, to Mexico. In New York he saw *A Majority of One* with Molly Picon and Cedric Hardwicke, which he decided played every bit as well as it read. He would do it in London. His television appearances were a great success and not nearly as hard work as he had feared. Of the Playhouse 90 production of Bernard Shaw's *Misalliance, Variety* reported: 'Morley, of course, stole the show, not only because he is a magnificent actor, but also because the part of the lusty and eccentric Englishman seems to have been written for him.' In the DuPont Show of the Month production of *Oliver Twist* Robert was Mr Brownslow — and a very sympathetic one.

He came back home to gather up Coral Browne and together they recreated *The Man Who Came to Dinner* for BBC radio, and then he compered an all-star bill at the Lyric Theatre to raise money for the Fréjus Flood Disaster Relief Fund. He also had a wonderful suggestion which he made in a letter to *The Times:* 'I understand that, during a recent tram strike in Hongkong, the employees continued to operate the services but refused to collect any money from the passengers. Might I suggest a similar compromise would benefit everyone if the threatened rail strike should take place here?'

Then Robert had his eyebrows manicured and played a Japanese business tycoon to Molly Picon's Jewish widow in *A Majority of One* at the Phoenix Theatre. The critics were certainly surprised. 'Morley with eyebrows thinned, face yellowed and the famous expressions disciplined, manages to convince us that, while still manifestly Robert Morley, he is also a Japanese textile tycoon.' W. A. Darlington thought it 'perhaps a pity that Mr Morley's comic gifts have to be suggested rather than exercised, but the part requires an actor of his calibre to indicate, under the mask of inscrutability, the gradual deepening of the feeling with which Mrs Jacoby (Molly Picon) inspires him.' Still, all those who had been previously somewhat condescending about Robert's dynamic stage presence rather missed it in this subdued performance.

Backstage, an electric cooker was installed in Robert's room and Ros was serving up fried fish and lamb croquettes cooked in the Jewish way under the inspiration of Molly.

175

While being an inscrutable oriental each night, by day Robert was back in his Oscar Wilde role — this time for a film. It was being made in a rush. His Wilde was being photographed in black and white and directed by Gregory Ratoff. At the same time another film about Wilde was being made in glorious technicolour by Warwick films, starring Peter Finch. Lawsuits were hurled back and forth while Robert got on with filming. His comment on the dispute was: 'I should have thought two films were better than one. I'd be quite happy to appear in both.'

Wilton, dressed in a sailor suit, had the role of one of Wilde's sons and for this he received a bicycle. Later he pointed out that it wasn't anywhere near as valuable as the Impressionist painting Annabel had received for her work in *Outcast of the Islands*. Robert told him she had a bigger part, and besides the Wilde picture was low budget — and Sheridan complained that he'd never even been in a movie.

Robert's film, called simply *Oscar Wilde,* beat the Finch film, *The Trials of Oscar Wilde* (in America it was called *The Green Carnation*) to the screen by three days, and opened with a charity premiere in aid of the Moroccan Earthquake Relief Fund on May 22nd, 1960. 'The court records write Morley a far better script than (does) Jo Eisinger — and here he comes into his own as his Wilde wilts under the merciless examination of Sir Ralph Richardson's Carson. This is a conflict of giants and I watched horrified and with growing pity as Wilde's epigrams flash less brilliantly as his responses turn against him, as his jewelled banter becomes plain and incriminating admissions, as he finally traps himself and is beaten to the ground by the advocate.'

Robert himself has said that he was ten years too young the first time he played Wilde and ten years too old the second time.

By the end of October he was back in New York. He made some of his many appearances on *The Jack Paar Show,* talking to Eleanor Roosevelt one night and Bobby Kennedy the next. It was the run-up to the American elections and Robert went in a motorcade to the big Kennedy rally. He was

The gourmet Max in Too Many Chefs

Joan and Robert with Daisy, 1978

rather pleased when Jack Kennedy came up to him after the rally to say how much Jackie had enjoyed Robert's television appearances. If he could have voted for him he certainly would have — such manners and tact! After taping the Paar show with Bobby they all went on to dine at the 21 night-club as Ethel Kennedy was keen to see the show in colour, and there was a television set there.

After New York Robert flew to Rome to play Potiphar in *Joseph and his Brethren,* which after looking at himself costumed in strange dresses, odd hats and jewelled chokers, he decided was rather a Peter Bull part. He searched a good deal for the Dolce Vita which was supposed to be raging but decided it all came down to men in dark glasses in night-clubs sharing one girl between two for the evening because most parents wouldn't allow their daughters out.

Throughout the filming, he worked on scripts for a television series he had devised for ATV called *If the Crown Fits.* He was to play King Rupert of Grabnia — a mythical kingdom somewhere in the Mediterranean. Peter Bull, who played his Major Domo, recalls that never before or since had there been so much channel switching over to BBC. Tracy Reed played Robert's daughter; Robert Hardy was his public relations man, and for one episode Gladys Cooper played, rather improbably, a working ballerina, Madam Olga. When Peter pointed out that although the casting was a bit strange and that the scripts hadn't even been written, Gladys as a ballerina was really going too far, Robert said, 'Nonsense — it will keep her out of trouble.' *Punch* reported the disaster: 'The first sight of Robert Morley's series *If the Crown Fits* hit me pretty hard. Experience has made me television-wary and it is some time since I watched humour so ponderous or comedy that creaked so like a bullock-cart. Peter Bull, I'm sure, has grounds for civil action over the lines he was lumbered with. Two jolly quips which haunt me — and probably him — will give non-viewers an idea of the hilarity afoot. In reading a message without his glasses, he reported, "There was an indecent at the frontier this morning — I'm sorry, the word should be incident" and

177

"Karl Marx? Is he the one who plays the harp?"'

Perhaps to forget it all, Robert threw himself into work at the film studios that summer. He made *The Young Ones* with pop star Cliff Richard, *Go To Blazes,* and joined Hope and Crosby on *The Road To Hongkong*. Then, pausing briefly to play Mr Rhodes in a play of the same name by Ronald Gow at the Theatre Royal, Windsor, for his old friend John Counsell, he flew to India to film again — this time a picture about the assassination of Gandhi called *Nine Hours To Rama*. He spent a good deal of his time in New Delhi being measured for his costumes and startling the local tailors, who weren't accustomed to such dimensions. He took a keen interest in fake jewellery and haggling in bazaars as there wasn't much else to do except watch the director trying to get the right atmosphere. The actor playing Gandhi was a look-alike amateur who was doing the film for love while everyone else got paid. The other Indians used to torture him by talking about buying houses in Kensington Gore. And despte the keen search for verisimilitude, the scene of the assassination was moved from the front of the house to the back garden so the roses wouldn't get trampled. Robert just made it home in time for Christmas.

One of the last projects of the Robin Fox Partnership was *A Time To Laugh*. Written by Robert Crean, an American television playwright, this was his first attempt at a stage play. It was set in the West Indies at the winter home of a religiously maniacal, fabulously rich Papal Countess who took to weaving hair shirts and delighting more in the paraphernalia of Roman Catholicism than in its substance. Also present was her frustrated daughter, a renegade priest, a mad maid and a visiting bishop to sort out the mess that transpires. Tyrone Guthrie, who had recently been knighted and was about to set out for Minneapolis as artistic director of the theatre there, agreed to direct Robert as the worldly-wise bishop and Ruth Gordon as the mad American lady. Michael Blakemore, who had left Australia as Robert had bid him and gone to RADA before embarking on a career in the theatre, was cast as Robert's priest secretary. Robert had

178

indeed been keeping, as he had promised Michael's father, an eye on him since his arrival in England. When beginning as an actor, at a miserably low salary he had lent Michael some money. Michael was repaying on the instalment plan but when he arrived in Robert's dressing-room backstage during the run of *The Little Hut* with ten hard-saved pounds on account, Robert seemed so surprised by the payment Michael never bothered to save up the rest. Rehearsals were as ever a delight though Guthrie was suffering from sinusitis. 'That was very good Robert,' he would say, 'but it was very slow. That was comedy 1910 and we are living in the sixties. If we could do it once again and twice as fast?'

Robert strove to please him — and he did. But soon the optimism faded. They opened in Oxford and the audiences didn't know what to make of the play. Ruth Gordon tried to quit and Robert, as part of the management and also knowing he was rather good as the bishop, spent a good deal of time placating her, hoping that they could make the rather disjointed play work. Robin was never very optimistic about their chances. *A Time To Laugh* opened at The Piccadilly Theatre on April 24th, 1962. W. A. Darlington was the most charitable reviewer: 'Mr Crean has compounded the play out of a mixture of elements of which the most important is a deep religious sincerity: the others are comedy, flippancy amounting to an apparent blasphemy and a sense of eccentric character drawing. He keeps to himself as a secret the full seriousness of his intentions; and by the time he shows what he is after, the audience is in no mood to follow him.' Darlington also agreed with Robert about his performance as the bishop: 'He plays a dove-and-serpent bishop whose surface worldly-wisdom seems sometimes to lead to a shockingly materialistic humour, but proves to disguise real goodness. This is all magnificently rendered; a piece of acting to rank with Mr Morley's best.'

The play closed within three weeks.

CHAPTER TWELVE

DURING THE NEXT FIVE YEARS Robert made twenty films — some notable, others not so. There was *The Old Dark House*, a comedy-horror film where he worked again with Peter Bull, taking him out to lunch to bribe him for his good lines. 'I hate my line,' he would say to Bull over the smoked salmon. 'Give me your line.' As often as not he got it.

Filming, he always thought, was a marvellous way to see the world at someone else's expense and in August 1963 he set off for Istanbul by way of Athens. There was a champagne and caviar lunch on the plane but Robert was dieting again and settled for an apple. The diet however was short-lived in the face of Turkish hospitality — fried aubergines, chicken with peaches, and gorgeous cheeses. At first Robert stayed at the Istanbul Hilton and had a balcony overlooking the Bosphorus. He took endless trips in steamers to the islands and watched Peter Ustinov arriving for the filming in his yacht. A good deal of the action for the film, *Topkapi*, took place on the roof of the museum from which the crooks are stealing a jewelled dagger. Robert spent four days watching everyone else up on the roof as he, ever afraid of heights, had talked himself out of that sequence. By this time he had moved to the Cinar Hotel. No matter how happy he finds himself in his first choice there always lurks in Robert's mind the suspicion that around the corner or across the town is a far superior accommodation waiting for him, so he packs his bags and moves.

180

As Ustinov, Melina Mercouri, and the director Jules Dassin spent all their free time socializing in French, Robert rather took to spending his time with the Turks, who conversed in English. He joined them at the races and for bridge games as well as continually exploring the beaches and bazaars. Robin flew out to join him, as Robert was, after many weeks in Turkey, rather homesick. He arrived just in time for an earthquake which Robert slept through. In his search for a romantic encounter Robin met a Turkish rug seller who kept promising him introductions. Robert refused to believe the rug man's yarns of his sexual prowess. 'The only thing he ever laid,' Robert told Robin, 'was a carpet. Be careful you're not landed with one.'

Ghengis Khan took him to Belgrade where he had great fun on the buses and trains exploring Yugoslavia and sharing grapes and cheese with the locals who all thought they had seen him somewhere before. *The Loved One* took him back to California, where Gladys was once more in residence. Tony Richardson, the director thought it would be terribly amusing if Robert dressed up in black leather for his part in the Waugh classic, but Robert demurred and thought that garb more appropriate for Liberace. 'What a wonderful idea,—' Richardson thought, and found a part for him. *Tendre Voyou* with Jean-Paul Belmondo took him to Tahiti where he visited the Gauguin Museum (although it didn't have any of his paintings) and numerous monuments to Captain Cook, who seemed to have landed on every beach.

While relentless filming continued in Paris, London or California, everyone kept telling Robert it was time he did a play again. Sewell was sure he would never again get into the discipline of nightly performances. No script presented itself to Robert's satisfaction. He rather fancied the idea of a one man show. Emlyn Williams managed to go around the world very nicely as Dickens or Dylan Thomas. A one man show meant you could write your own plane tickets and go where you chose rather than waiting for a film company to choose a location that was interesting. But Robert would have to be himself — that version of himself that he had heightened into

181

a performance. He devised *The Sound of Morley*. Australia was the place to do it, he decided, and gathering up Tom Chatto to see him through it, they set off for Sydney. There was a good deal of the Odd Couple about the tour as they bickered about who was to open the garage door or put the kettle on for tea, but Robert found that Australia had improved a good deal in seventeen years — although he still wasn't quite sure about Melbourne. The show worked very well, except that Robert soon began to dread stepping on stage, knowing he was going to be there all by himself for two hours.

During the previous years, when Robert was home at Fairmans — in between films — he and Sewell had begun working together on a reluctant autobiography called *Robert Morley: Responsible Gentleman,* after the parts he had played early in his career, and he took a flying promotion tour around America signing the books — 'In memory of Capri' or 'If only we could have it all again', — for the startled customers who had asked for his autograph.

Back in London he at last found a play he thought would work. Peter Ustinov's play *Halfway Up The Tree* had Robert as a retired general from the British Army who becomes a hippie drop-out. Binkie Beaumont was presenting it. He rang up Ambrosine Phillpotts from Paris where he was with Peter Ustinov and John Gielgud, who was to direct it, and told her 'Robert is dead keen to have you in it. You just have to convince Peter Ustinov and John. Would you mind reading it for them?' Ambrosine did not mind, and once again, after an interval of twenty-five years, she was playing Robert's wife. They toured it briefly in England and for the premiere in Manchester, to celebrate Robert's return to the stage, Sheridan's son, Hugo, was born on October 2nd, 1967. Robert took great delight in being a grandfather and decided that Hugo was a good omen for the play. *Halfway Up The Tree* opened in London on November 23rd, 1967. Irving Wardle in *The Times* said: 'The main justification for this play is that it tempted Robert Morley back on the London stage.' In Paris and New York the play, without Robert as the eccentric General Sir Mallalieu FitzButtress, failed to last but it ran in London for a year at the Queen's Theatre. Peter Ustinov was never quite sure whether he preferred the play done the way he had written it and not quite lasting, or having it done with Robert's rewriting and being a hit.

Always happiest in the role of host, Robert gave his own sixtieth birthday party and flew a large number of family and friends to Le Touquet, the Normandy resort which was virtually closed because it was the time of the French general strikes. The airport was actually closed but luckily there were no other planes about so the party landed safely. The group numbered twenty-eight — the youngest member was nine months and the eldest nearly eighty. A walk on the grey, deserted beach was followed by a massive lunch topped by strawberries and mountainous meringues at Flavio's Restaurant. Then there were electric go-cart rides through the empty streets with Gladys more than once mounting the pavements. A quick trip to the Casino, then a flight home as the rain began. At no point did anyone remember to sing 'Happy Birthday to You.'

That autumn he tried once again to go to China — for years every birthday he had vowed that this would be the year, and once again he was defeated in his efforts to obtain a visa. Russia would have to do, and a trip on the Trans-Siberian railway. Always a socialist, Robert believes that all Russians are equal and immensely happy, and has a romantic notion that the West will come round to communism. Modified, of course, so that he can go on having a pool, an expense account and the Order of Lenin. A series of columns on his adventures for the London *Evening News* would help pay for the expedition, and Sheridan went along part of the way to take some pictures. Robert found none of the intrigue he had expected on the railway and went on to Japan where he found lots of decorations for Christmas.

Christmas always transforms Fairmans into — well, Christmas always transforms Fairmans. Robert tacks Christmas cards to the beams, angels to the window frames, hangs massive gaudy balls from the lamps, and puts tinsel on anything that stands still.

'Well, what do you think?' He surveys his efforts with pride.

'It looks rather like a down-market department store.'

'Exactly,' he replies, 'the effect I was striving for.'

There then follows the ritual argument over whether the lights go on the Christmas tree before or after the decorations.

Although he's been a big success on television chat shows in both America and England, and also in games (*What's My Line* and *Call My Bluff*), Robert had still to conquer situation comedy — so in January 1969 he decided to have another try. Together with Jeremy Paul he wrote a series called *Charge* about Herbert Todhunter, a prejudiced, ignorant and distrustful member of the lower-upper classes who lives on a houseboat with his friend and stooge, Partridge. Robert, of course, played Todhunter, and Robert Raglan his friend. This time it was at the BBC's expense but the results were far from spectacular. The *Sunday Times* reported: 'Now it is a fact that when Mr Morley finds himself the guest on a chat show he is always great fun, rattling on in his quirky way with small respect for progressive sensibilities, which are always so tender (though I suspect his heart is in the right place). All the more surprising then, that in this contrived show the jokes were few and feeble, the pace funereal, and the punches not merely telegraphed but notified by semaphore.'

Robert, larger than life, just could not fit his characters into a television studio. Much more successful was his look at public school life called 'Was your schoolmaster really necessary?' in the series *One Pair of Eyes* — also done for the BBC. The *Daily Mail* said: 'Morley could so easily have fallen into the trap of overpontificating on the evils of public schools: instead he was so amiable and receptive it was almost impossible not to be won over.'

In 1969 there was a trip to the remote island of Mull filming *When Eight Bells Toll* and to the wilds of Buckinghamshire for *Cromwell*. Here he narrowly missed having to ride a horse. Robert loves racing; he loves owning racehorses; but he keeps his distance from them even when leading them into the winners' circle.

There was a quick trip to Las Vegas while his first granddaughter, Alexis, was being born. Although manifesting an enormous interest in most things, the actual process of birth is one that Robert has studiously avoided many times. He adores witnessing the new arrival — but preferably tidily wrapped up in swaddling clothes and lying if not in a manger at least in a cot. This is a characteristic he shared with his father-in-law, Buck, who walked him resolutely up and down the road outside Fairmans while Wilton was coming into the world — even though it was barely dawn. The mystery of birth is the one that Robert prefers to leave unsolved.

He began rehearsals for his next play on his birthday. Rehearsals were to be held at the Irish Club and Robert despaired when the press photographers were invited to watch him cut the cake — anything more boring than a picture of him cutting a birthday cake he could not imagine. Yet he posed and smiled and wished rehearsals were all over. It was bad enough to have to rehearse, but in rooms, rather than on a stage where there could be a polite distance between the director and himself, it was excruciating. This time the play was by Alan Ayckbourn, called *How the Other Half Loves*. And this time the producers were Peter Bridge and Eddie Kulukundis. Robert had quarrelled with Binkie Beaumont, — though not about the theatre; where professionalism was concerned they still had a great respect for each other. But Robert had been raising money for a school for autistic children. This was a charity very close to Robert's heart. He had always been amazed by and grateful for his own children; he had also believed that learning to communicate, to express themselves, was the most important thing. He wanted to help children who couldn't. He needed about £50,000 and approached all his friends for sizable donations, most of whom obliged. But Binkie refused. In an attempt to break him down Robert actually staged a sit-in in Beaumont's office for two days. But to no avail.

185

Alan Ayckbourn had written his comedy for the theatre at Scarborough where he was resident dramatist and there it consisted of a six-sided triangle; three couples interacting in equal proportions. Well, Robert was bound to overbalance it and he did, to Ayckbourn's dismay, but the play was still a delight. Joan Tetzel had once again materialized from America as if by magic and played his wife. They came to London the first week of August 1970. Frank Marcus, himself a playwright, wrote in the *Sunday Telegraph:* 'The play has both lost and gained. It has lost its symmetry. Instead of six equally important characters, we have the over-powering presence of Mr Morley himself. Speaking — if memory serves me right — his own rather than the author's dialogue, he is like a turtle in a fish tank, imposing his rhythm on the environment and making the others tremble in his ripples . . . So what have we got? An adroit farce — quite the funniest now playing in London — and an irresistible bravura performance from Mr Morley: bright and elated like a gorgeous balloon but tethered very uncertainly in reality.'

During rehearsals of *How The Other Half Loves* Robin Fox had been admitted to hospital in West Sussex. He had terminal cancer. There was absolutely no hope, but Robert tried to produce some, driving each evening after rehearsals with champagne to Robin's bedside and bringing him tales of the company and picnics from Fortnum's. Robin did not give in easily to his disease. He tried Dr. Issels's clinic in Bavaria and fought the cancer with the little strength he had left. Robert would fly out on Sundays to visit him there and wonder at the courage of his friend. But in January 1971 Robin died — and after twenty years of guidance, counsel, support and love, Robert missed him very much.

The year ended with another death. Gladys, touring England as Mrs St. Maugham in *The Chalk Garden* came down with pneumonia. Throughout their relationship, Robert had been constantly impressed by what he termed her courage and style, and none of it deserted her in her last hours. It took a great effort but she got out of bed and made

186

her way to her dressing-table where she brushed her hair and, looking in the mirror at the very famous face which had graced many hundreds of postcards, said, 'If this is what virus pneumonia does to one, I really don't think I shall bother to have it again.' She died that night in her sleep a few weeks before what would have been her eighty-third birthday.

How The Other Half Loves ran at the Lyric for two years. There were no dinners cooked backstage every Saturday now — Ros was busy being Robert's agent. But she did manage to organize the constant parties that Robert found excuses for. During the run Robert turned even more to the journalism he so enjoys. He was writing articles for *The Tatler, Punch, Playboy* and various newspapers. Also over the years editors with a couple of inches to fill had learned that a quick phone call to Robert would give them a joke, or a neat piece of controversy to tidy up the space.

It was also at this time that Robert was approached by the advertising representatives of British Airways, then still calling themselves BOAC. Would Mr Morley consent to making some advertisements for the United States? Gladly, Robert agreed. He was then told filming would begin in two days' time — and he got suspicious.

'Who turned you down?' Robert asked them.

'Why, no one,' they assured him. 'You were our first choice.'

Robert didn't press the issue but he had been in the business long enough to know full well that the filming wouldn't have been organized just on speculation. Months later he learned that Laurence Olivier had been their first choice — but Robert was rather pleased. No shame at all in picking up after Olivier.

He went into the advertising campaign with all the gusto of having found a new toy. He began watching other people's commercials with a searching eye. The storyboard he was presented with became the starting point for ideas he had thought up, and wittier lines, and soon he was selling British Airways with all the enthusiasm and expertise he had used

187

for years in selling himself. The effort was worthwhile. British Airways increased their share of the Atlantic market immensely.

While Robert stayed on at the Lyric the cast began to change around him. Young actors were no longer prepared to stay in a long run — something Robert has never been able to understand. To him, each audience is new and fresh and it is a challenge to make them laugh. If anything, a long run only makes him more inventive — of course, if everyone on stage was going around being creative only chaos would result. And Robert liked to keep a firm hand on the play. It was all right for him to experiment with the laughs, but not for everyone. Ian McCulloch replaced Donald Burton as the young man who was having an affair with Robert's wife — and had some of his own ideas about what was funny on stage. At one point he introduced a raucous belch. Robert didn't approve and told him not to do it again.

'But it's funny,' Ian told him.

'Well,' Robert said, 'Robin Midgely [the director] wouldn't like it.'

'He thinks it's funny too.'

'Alan Ayckbourn wouldn't like it.'

'Yes he does,' Ian countered.

'Well,' Robert searched desperately for someone who would back him up. 'Joan wouldn't approve.' And that was the last word.

The company took the play to Toronto and then Robert went off to Australia to do a tour of it with an Australian cast. Annabel accompanied him and joined him for a very social two months before Joan and Wilton flew out. Joan spent the time catching up on very old friendships they had forged during *Edward, My Son* and Wilton was so taken by Australia that he decided to stay and eventually started his own theatrical production company which he called Parachute Productions — 'One drop and we fold.'

Robert had another idea for a play — a comedy about death and dying, entitled *Ghost on Tiptoe*. Rosemary Anne Sisson worked on it with him, and once more Ambrosine played his wife. When they opened in Birmingham the first night ran nearly three hours. There were in fact two plays there — one a rather sophisticated comedy about life and death, and the other a farce. Robert decided, encouraged by Ray Cooney who was producing, to extract the farce and bring that to London. Robert played a businessman who, when told he has a year to live, rehearses the reading of his will, orders drinks for the wake, begins to paint ridiculous canvases, keeps a bat for a pet, cooks bouillabaisse for the family with goldfish, and threatens to go to South America with a hippie. It gave him the opportunity to dress in a variety of different and bizarre costumes.

They opened in May at the Savoy and Jeremy Kingston reported in *Punch:* 'Robert Morley is hard to resist: a powerful personality, always fun to watch and nearly always worth watching. He stomps about the stage, heaving himself from chair to sofa, crushing the spirit out of defenceless cushions . . . but the plays he now stars in tend to be less sturdy than he, and this is a pity. He has always disparaged his abilities, holding them, like Coward, to be little more than "a talent to amuse". But he does also have a talent to move, which his plays permit him to exercise just once or twice but never more often.'

A Ghost On Tiptoe was exhausting for Robert. It was true the play was merely a framework within which he played out various scenes at breakneck speed. William Franklyn, as his solicitor, had a few good lines but the show rested on Robert completely.

Ambrosine became fed up with standing around the stage with nothing to do but be a stooge, as she had years before in *Play with Fire*. Besides Robert kept baiting her — some nights he would do a scene very, very fast, prodding Ambrosine to keep up with him. She deliberately went even more slowly. And she was incensed that whenever Robert thought up a new funny line he invariably gave it to Joyce Carey who was playing his mother. Ambrosine thought he was behaving very badly and told him so. He stopped visiting her dressing-room. But finally they reached the end of the year's run.

189

'Well, Ambrose,' he said, going into her dressing-room after the curtain fell for the last time, 'we've managed it; we're still together. Come on, let's go out to supper.' He was off the next morning bright and early for Mexico, but that was tomorrow. Ambrosine was going into a nursing home for a rest. She said no. He walked her to her car. 'What would you say if I offered you a play in let's say four years' time?' Ambrosine couldn't believe it. Three hours before they had hardly been speaking. She just looked at him coolly. 'Let's make a date,' she said. The next morning she found flowers from him in her room when she arrived. It was impossible to stay cross with Robert and she had certainly tried.

The following Christmas Robert's second granddaughter was born. He and Hugo decided to take their minds off the ordeal with a matinee of *Treasure Island*.

By this time Robert felt that all the Americans he had persuaded to fly to England on British Airways expected to find him in residence at a theatre in the West End, and he didn't want to disappoint them. He looked around for another play to do — one that wouldn't be quite such hard work as *A Ghost On Tiptoe,* and he settled on a revival of a solidly-constructed farce by Ben Travers called *Banana Ridge*. Although it gave him plenty of scope, it also had other strong characters and there was time during the action when he could put his feet up in his dressing-room and watch his mini-television. *Banana Ridge* opened, back at the Savoy, the last week of July 1976. Benny Green, writing in *Punch,* said, 'People will come to see Morley striding through the Malayan undergrowth wearing khaki shorts, green woollen socks, brown suede boots and a hat which looks as though it has escaped from a touring production of *Beau Geste.* They will come to watch him trying to operate a home-made soda siphon which makes a naughty noise when the nozzle is pressed. They will come to see him peer morbidly at large tumblers containing microscopic measures of diluted whisky. Morley is a pastmaster at this sort of thing, and though it is received opinion to say that when on stage he merely plays himself, there is some evidence that effective

190

comic performances as he gives them are not as easily achieved as all that.'

That autumn, for the first time Robert walked down the aisle. The bride on his arm was his daughter Annabel. In the little church in Wargrave where she had been christened she was marrying Charles Little, an Australian actor. The wedding was in the morning and a large marquee at Fairmans held hundreds of friends and relatives for lunch, but Robert couldn't stay for the speeches. He had a matinee at the Savoy.

Halfway through the run of *Banana Ridge* Julian Orchard replaced George Cole in the part of Robert's down-trodden employee on the rubber plantation. Julian hadn't worked with Robert since the days of *Fanny,* and had been very much looking forward to it. It was great fun being back on stage with Robert, and most Saturdays, between the shows, he joined Robert and Sewell down the Strand at Simpsons for a meal, when Robert would regale them with tales of his travels and his hopes for the future.

'But Robert,' Julian would counter, 'you can't believe in communism — you own a race horse.'

'If they didn't want people to own race horses they would bring in a law to stop it,' Robert explained. 'There's nothing privileged about owning race horses — anyone can.'

Julian felt there was something intrinsically wrong with that argument but Robert's romantic vision was unshakable.

Working with Robert could be unpredictable, and there were occasions when Julian regretted the experience. Twice in one week Robert had missed an entrance. It was a scene in which Julian had to make a breathless change and then stand ready to greet his employer. He hurried through the change and stood there — and waited and waited. The first time, Robert had found himself on television playing Louis XI in an old film — *The Adventures of Quentin Durward;* the second occasion Lester Piggott was in a big race. Julian left the stage and met Robert in the wings.

'If you have a moment, Robert,' he said with all the

191

sarcasm he could muster. They went on stage together and cobbled up the edges, but Julian was white and shaking with anger. He was so furious he couldn't speak. While he was waiting in the wings for his next entrance Robert went up to him.

'I'm so sorry dear,' he said, 'but you know the trouble with you? The trouble with you is that you are a creature of habit.' Then he went on stage leaving Julian to miss his entrance he was so convulsed with laughter. They were about to start the matinee one day when a letter was delivered to Julian as they waited in the wings. Ever curious, Robert perked up. 'What's that?'

'Wait a minute, I haven't even opened it.' Julian opened it and found it was from the man who was going to direct his Christmas pantomime at Croydon. He was in the audience that day and looking forward to meeting him after the performance.

'May I see it?' Robert asked. He took the letter and looked at it. 'Ah, don't trust him, dear. People who haven't got addresses printed on their notepaper are about to move.'

Julian thought he must be performing with Oscar Wilde that afternoon.

That summer the holiday was in Brittany. Every morning he would take Juliet, then eighteen months, to explore the sand and paddle in the sea. Often in the afternoon he holed up and rehearsed his one man show in the garage, because he was going to have another try. He did actually perform it for a couple of weeks in Brighton and Richmond, but every performance was agony — not only because he missed the camaraderie of other actors but because it was a very personal show. He talked of his family and his life; he performed the last scene from *Oscar Wilde* and, as Michael Blakemore (now a respected director) said when he saw it, 'Robert paid the audience the tribute of treating them as friends.' Every night, though, Robert had to be steered onto the stage — like that first night in New York as he sat in Rumplemeyers, he wondered if he should run away. He stayed the course but couldn't contemplate going on with it.

The filming of *Too Many Chefs,* a comedy-thriller, took him to some of the best restaurants on the continent. It also gave him the best film part he had had in years. The role of Maximillian Vandervere could very well have been written with Robert in mind. Max is the editor of a food magazine; he is both a gourmet and a gourmand — and Robert followed his stomach into every frame. 'My body,' he declared, 'is my work of art.' Then after Christmas he decided it was time to introduce Hugo to the realities of work, and together they filmed a commercial for British Airways on board the *Queen Elizabeth II.* With Hugo and Alexis he spent a week being cosseted at Disney World in Florida — what an ideal place to live, he thought, and such an interesting address — then Robert flew off to Australia (via Las Vegas, which wasn't remotely on the way) to make a commercial for Heinz and to visit Wilton who had bought a house there and was flourishing.

Robert was back well in time for the birth of Annabel's daughter. Annabel's husband, being of the modern school, was very keen on the mechanics of the whole scene and kept describing the progress graphically. Robert couldn't bear it. 'Sewell and I,' he told him 'have remained innocents.' What his bachelor friend Sewell had to do with it no one quite understood. But Robert was soon hurrying to the hospital to view the baby, called Daisy.

'Your first grandchild?' the nurse asked.

'Yes, yes indeed,' he told her untruthfully. 'Well,' he explained when challenged by Joan, 'I thought it made me sound younger.' Then, having found the birth a great strain, he hurried off to the airport to catch a plane. He wasn't particular where it went and was horrified to find that there weren't many going any place from Heathrow at four o'clock in the afternoon. But finally he arrived in Nice where he headed for the Casino. It was in a way his method of giving thanks for the safe arrival. If he was going to remain lucky in life it was helpful if he was a totally unsuccessful gambler. Sacrifices must be made to propitiate the fates — and he was prepared to sacrifice money. Everything else was going

193

nicely. As Rex Harrison (who had been through a number of wives and homes since *Short Story*) had summed it up one afternoon when they met by chance in the Burlington Arcade: 'Ah Robert, one wife, one house — one performance.'

It was time for another play. Robert had become fascinated with transvestism. In Australia Wilton had been producing a tour of *The Elocution of Benjamin Franklin,* a one man show about the subject starring Gordon Chater. Robert had dinner with the adviser to the show and was slightly amazed when he came in full drag. Robert then decided on his next play. John Wells joined him in Berkshire to help him write it. Three married men, all happily heterosexual, also happen to like dressing up in women's clothes on occasion. Robert, playing a high court judge, was one of them. They opened the play in Birmingham.

'What am I doing?' Robert asked backstage, applying blue eyeshadow and rapidly approaching his seventieth birthday. 'Do I really need all this?' He had been busily rewriting and re-rehearsing all week. *A Picture of Innocence* was taking shape. 'I suppose,' he decided, 'it's become a habit.' A habit indeed — going on stage every night and making people laugh. Friends and critics over the years had often complained that Robert hadn't approached the classics and serious drama. He certainly had the ability, but not the inclination. He much preferred an audience with tears of laughter running from their eyes to one with just the tears.

His seventieth birthday would be celebrated at home with a few old friends and then he was off to Toronto for a month with the new play. On the flight without a doubt someone would stop him and say — 'Why, it is Mr British Airways.' A roundabout way, perhaps, but Robert had indeed become 'something in the Empire'. His mother would have been pleased.

BIBLIOGRAPHY

Acton, Harold, *Nancy Mitford — A Memoir,* Hamish Hamilton, 1975

Barnes, Sir Kenneth, *Welcome Good Friends,* Peter Davis Ltd., 1958

Benchley, Nathaniel, *Humphrey Bogart,* Hutchinson, 1975

Bishop, C. H., *Folkestone, The Story of a Town,* Headley Brothers Ltd., 1973

Bolitho, Hector, *Marie Tempest,* Cobden-Sanderson, 1936

Braun, Eric, *Deborah Kerr,* W. H. Allen, 1977

Bull, Peter, *I Know the Face But,* Peter Davies, 1959

Bull, Peter, *I Say, Look Here!,* Peter Davies, 1965

Counsell, John, *Counsell's Opinion,* Barrie & Rockliff, 1963

Darlington, W. A., *Six Thousand and One Nights — Forty Years A Critic,* George G. Harrap & Co. Ltd., 1960

Forsyth, James, *Tyrone Guthrie,* Hamish Hamilton, 1976

Gielgud, John, *Distinguished Company,* Heinemann, 1972

Guthrie, Tyrone, *A Life in the Theatre,* Hamish Hamilton, 1959

Harrison, Rex, *Rex — An Autobiography,* MacMillan, London, 1974

Hartnoll, Phyliss, *The Oxford Companion to the Theatre*

Keown, Eric, *Margaret Rutherford,* Theatre World Monograph no. 7, Rockliff Press

Kulik, Karol, *Alexander Korda, The Man Who Could Work Miracles,* W. H. Allen, 1975

Lillie, Beatrice, *Every Other Inch a Lady,* W. H. Allen, 1973

Marshall, Norman, *The Other Theatre,* John Lehmann Ltd., 1947

Morley, Robert and Stokes, Sewell, *Robert Morley, Responsible Gentleman,* Heinemann, 1966

Morley, Robert, *A Musing Morley,* Robson Books Ltd., 1974

Morley, Robert, *Morley Marvels,* Robson Books Ltd., 1976

Morley, Robert, *Short Story,* H. F. W. Deane & Sons, 1936

Morley, Robert and Langley, Noel, *Edward, My Son,* Samuel French Ltd., 1948

Pearson, Hesketh, *The Last Actor Managers,* Methuen & Co. Ltd., 1950

Pascal, Valerie, *The Devil and His Disciple,* Michael Joseph, 1970

Rossi, Alfred, *Astonish Us In The Morning,* Hutchinson, 1977

Robyns, Gwen, *Margaret Rutherford,* W. H. Allen, 1972

Sherek, Henry, *Not In Front of the Children,* Heinemann, 1959

Stokes, Sewell and Leslie, *Oscar Wilde,* Martin Secker & Warburg Ltd., 1937

Swindell, Larry, *Spencer Tracy,* W. H. Allen, 1970

Tate, Viola, *A Family of Brothers - The Taits & J. C. Williamson, A Theatre History,* Heinemann, Melbourne, 1971

Trewin, J. C., *Peter Brook,* Macdonald & Co. Ltd., 1971

Trewin, J. C., *Robert Donat,* Heinemann, 1968

Thomas, Bob, *Thalberg - Life and Legend,* Doubleday & Co. Inc., 1969

Ustinov, Peter, *Dear Me,* Heinemann, 1977

Vanburgh, Irene, *To Tell My Story,* Hutchinson & Co.

Wilcox, Herbert, *Twenty-five Thousand Sunsets,* The Bodley Head, 1967

CAREER

Plays:

1929	Treasure Island
1929–1936	Touring; Playhouse Oxford; Festival Cambridge
1936	Perranporth
1936	Oscar Wilde
1937	The Great Romancer
1937	Perranporth
1937	Pygmalion
1938	Perranporth
1938	Oscar Wilde (in New York)
1939	Perranporth
1940	Play With Fire
1941–1943	The Man Who Came to Dinner
1944	Staff Dance
1945–1946	The First Gentleman
1947–1950	Edward, My Son (London, New York, Australia, New Zealand)
1950–1953	The Little Hut
1954	Hippo Dancing
1956	A Likely Tale
1956	Fanny
1957	Hook, Line and Sinker
1959	A Majority of One
1961	Mr. Rhodes

1962	A Time to Laugh
1967–1968	Halfway Up The Tree
1970–1972	How The Other Half Loves
1974	A Ghost on Tiptoe
1976	Banana Ridge
1978	Picture of Innocence

Plays directed:

1957	The Tunnel of Love
1957	The Full Treatment
1959	Once More With Feeling

Plays Written:

1935	Short Story
1937	Goodness How Sad!
1944	Staff Dance
1947	Edward, My Son (with Noel Langley)
1957	The Full Treatment (with Ronald Gow)
1957	Six Months' Grace (with Dundas Hamilton)
1974	A Ghost on Tiptoe (with Rosemary Anne Sisson)
1978	Picture of Innocence (with John Wells)

One Man Shows:

| 1966 | The Sound of Morley |
| 1977 | Robert Morley Talks to Everybody! |

Books Published:

1966	Robert Morley, Responsible Gentleman (with Sewell Stokes)
1974	A Musing Morley (collection)
1976	Morley Marvels (collection)
1978	More Morley (collection)

Films:

1938	Marie Antoinette
1940	You Will Remember
1941	Major Barbara
1942	This Was Paris
	The Big Blockade
	The Foreman went to France
	The Young Mr. Pitt
1945	I Live in Grosvenor Square
1948	The Ghosts of Berkeley Square
1949	The Small Back Room
1951	Outcast of the Islands
	The African Queen
1952	Curtain Up
1953	The Final Test
	The Story of Gilbert and Sullivan
	Melba
	Beat the Devil
1954	The Good Die Young
	The Rainbow Jacket
	Beau Brummell
1955	The Adventures of Quentin Durward
1956	Loser Takes All
	The Sheriff of Fractured Jaw
	Around the World in Eighty Days
1959	The Journey
	The Doctor's Dilemma
	Libel
1960	The Battle of the Sexes
	Oscar Wilde
1961	Joseph and His Brethren
	The Young Ones
1962	Go To Blazes
	The Road to Hongkong
	The Boys

1963	Nine Hours to Rama
	Murder at the Gallop
	Ladies Who Do
	The Old Dark House
	Take Her She's Mine
1964	Hot Enough for June
	Of Human Bondage
	Topkapi
1965	Ghengis Khan
	Those Magnificent Men in Their Flying Machines
	A Study in Terror
1966	The Alphabet Murders
	Life at the Top
	The Loved One
	Hotel Paradiso
	Way Way Out
	Tendre Voyou
	Finders Keepers
1967	The Trygon Factor
	Woman Times Seven
1968	Hot Millions
1969	Some Girls Do
	Sinful Davy
1970	Twinky
	Doctor in Trouble
	Cromwell
	Song of Norway
1971	When Eight Bells Toll
1973	Theatre of Blood
1974	Great Expectations
1976	The Bluebird
1978	Too Many Chefs

INDEX

Abbott, George, 71
Adrian, Max, 68
The Adventures of Quentin Durward,
  162, 191
The African Queen, 150, 151
Agate, James, 106
Albery, Bronson, 48, 49
Allen, Adrianne, 122, 123
Amis, Kingsley, 169
And So To Bed, 29
Arms And The Man, 29
Arnaud, Yvonne, 158, 169
Arthur, Jean, 124
Ashcroft, Peggy, 111-12, 113, 114,
  117, 118, 120, 121, 122
Ashmore, Peter, 110, 113, 121, 159,
  164
Asquith, Anthony, 153, 172, 173
Astaire, Fred, 57
Astor, Lord, 20
Atkinson, Brooks, 67
Attlee, Clement, 119
Ayckbourn, Alan, 185, 186, 188

Bacall, Lauren, 150
Balmain, Pierre, 145
Banana Ridge, 190-2
Banbury, Frith, 50, 68
Bankhead, Tallulah, 66
Banzie, Brenda de, 158-9
Barber, John, 170
Barker, Felix, 172
Barnes, Kenneth, 23, 24, 26, 27, 138
Barrymore, Ethel, 119
Barrymore, John, 77
Bartholomew, Freddie, 62
Bartley, Tony, 172
Barton, Mary, 23

The Battle of the Sexes, 173
Baxter, Beverly, 114
Beat the Devil, 154-6, 157
Beaton, Cecil, 168
Beau Brummell, 161-2
Beaumont, Binkie, 35, 36, 100-1, 104,
  144, 145, 158, 182, 185
Beerbohm Tree, Sir Herbert, 22-3
Bellow, Kyrle, 25
Benson, Sir Frank, 31
Bergner, Elizabeth, 68
Betts, Ernest, 91, 97
Beverly, Miss (matron at Wellesley
  House), 17
The Big Blockade, 94
Blakemore, Michael, 131-2, 134, 135,
  136, 137-8, 178-9, 192
Bogarde, Dirk, 172, 173
Bogart, Humphrey, 150, 154, 156
Bourchier, Arthur, 24-5
Boyer, Charles, 122
Brennan, Walter, 75
British Airways commercials, 187-8,
  193
Brook, Clive, 109
Brook, Peter, 141-2, 144-5
Brown, Pamela, 63, 76
Browne, Coral, 49, 95, 96, 98, 175
Browne, W. Graham, 38
Brynner, Yul, 170-1
Buckmaster, Captain Herbert ('Buck')
  and Grace, 77-8, 79, 81, 85, 184
Buckmaster, Joan *see* Morley, Joan
Buckmaster, John, 69, 72, 74, 77-8,
  81, 83, 96
Bull, Peter, 31-2, 33, 40-2, 43, 50, 56,
  57-60, 61, 62-3, 67-8, 71, 78, 80, 82,
  96-7, 109, 143, 177, 180

Burton, Sir Montague, 117

Cadbury, Peter, 153
Campbell, Charles, 24
Capote, Truman, 155
Carey, Joyce, 189
Carmichael, Ian, 170
Carroll, John, 93
Cass, Henry, 89, 91
Chamberlain, Neville, 64, 65, 70, 72, 79, 80
Chapman, Alan, 138
Chaplin, Charlie, 57
Chappell, William, 147
Charge, 184
Chatto, Rosalind, 147, 166, 169-70, 187
Chatto, Tom, 170, 182
Chester, Elsie, 25
Churchill, Sarah, 80, 106
Churchill, Winston, 106
Clark, Leslie, 20
Clements, John, 117, 170
Collett, Richard, 73
Collier, Constance, 119
Conrad, Joseph, 148
Cooney, Ray, 189
Cooper, Gerald, 44
Cooper, Gladys, 72, 74, 80, 83, 104, 117, 118, 119, 120, 121, 123, 128, 129, 142, 144, 148, 153-4, 177, 186-7
Cooper, Sally, 162
Coward, Noël, 144, 156, 160
Crawford, Joan, 57, 60, 70
Crean, Robert, 178, 179
Cromwell, 184
Cruickshank, Alec, 104
Cukor, George, 117
Curtain Up, 152

Dare, Zena, 124
Darlington, W.A., 48, 68-9, 170, 173, 175, 179
Dassin, Jules, 181
Davis, Bette, 75
De Bear, Archie, 69
Dietrich, Marlene, 57, 92, 160
Doctor Knock, 77, 78
Dr Syn, 28, 29
The Doctor's Dilemma, 172, 173

Donat, Robert, 33, 97, 109
Douglas, Lord Alfred, 44
Du Maurier, Sir Gerald, 25, 27, 72

Edward My Son, 106, 108-9, 110-18, 119-27, 129, 131, 134, 138, 140-1, 156, 162-3
Elizabeth II, Queen, 108, 157, 160, 161, 168
Elliott, Canon Wallace, Harold, 15, 160
ENSA tour (1943), 99-100
Evans, Edith, 156

'Fairmans' (Morley's cottage at Wargrave), 85, 87, 89, 90, 91, 92-3, 94, 95, 96, 101, 104, 108, 118, 126, 147, 149, 151, 153, 164, 167, 183-4
Fanny, 165-8, 169
Farebrother, Violet, 164
Fass family, 10, 11
Fields, Gracie, 124
Fillipi, Rosina, 26
The Final Test, 156
Finch, Peter, 176
The First Gentleman, 88-9, 99, 103-8, 109, 110
Forbes-Robertson, Meriel, 32-4
Ford, Henry, 127
The Foreman Went to France, 94
Fox, Angela, 154, 155, 157, 172
Fox, Robin, 143, 154, 155, 157, 158, 159, 169-70, 172, 174, 181, 186
Franklin, Sidney, 55
Franklyn, William, 189
Frend, Charles, 94
The Full Treatment, 148, 154
Fulmer, Elroy, 128
Furse, Judith, 50, 68
Furse, Roger, 42, 63, 68

Gabor, Zsa-Zsa, 125
Garbo, Greta, 53, 70, 119
Garland, Judy, 62
Gay, John, 146
Ghengis Khan, 181
Ghost on Tiptoe, 188-90
Gielgud, John, 85, 86, 145, 156, 182
Gilbert, Nurse, 11
Gilliat, Sidney, 152

202

Ginsbury, Norman, 88-9, 103, 104-5
Gish, Dorothy, 122
Go To Blazes, 178
Goodness How Sad, 50, 59, 60, 63, 67-9, 71, 75, 80, 109
Gordon, Mary Lynn, 100
Gordon, Ruth, 178-9
Gottlieb, Morton, 129-30, 131-2, 134
Gow, Ronald, 148, 154, 178
Grant, Elspeth, 114
Gray, Terence, 30-1
The Great Romancer, 48-9, 95
Green, Benny, 190-1
Greene, Graham, 118, 119, 141
Guthrie, Tyrone, 35-7, 46, 51, 68, 178
Gwenn, Edmund, 119

Hale, Lionel, 51
Half an Hour, 29
Halfway Up The Tree, 182
Hamilton, Dundas, 169
Hamlet, 46, 51
Hammerstein, William, 165
Hanbury, Hilda, 143
Harding, Gilbert, 157
Hardwicke, Cedric, 124, 174
Hardy, Robert, 177
Harlow, John, 94
Harman, Jympson, 151
Harrison, Rex, 36, 37, 84, 102, 118, 123, 165, 194
Hay, Will, 94
Haye, Helen, 25, 26
Hayes, Helen, 62, 70
Hearst, Mrs Randolph, 124
Hellman, Lillian, 120
Hemingway, Ernest, 92
Hepburn, Katharine, 66, 150, 151
Hiller, Wendy, 86, 103, 105, 106, 121, 148
Hippo Dancing, 157, 158-60, 161, 162
Hitchcock, Alfred, 174
Hitler, Adolf, 65
Hobson, Harold, 115
Holm, Celeste, 120
Hook, Line and Sinker, 172-3
Hopper, Hedda, 61, 62
How The Other Half Loves, 185-7, 188
Howard, Zena, 159
Hunter, Hayes, 47, 51-2

Hunter, Ian, 109
Huston, John, 124, 150, 154-5, 157
Hyde-White, Wilfred, 99, 158-9, 160, 161, 162
Hylton, Jack, 116
Hyson, Dorothy, 82

I Live in Grosvenor Square, 102
If The Crown Fits, 177
The Importance of Being Earnest, 29, 50

The Jack Paar Show, 176
Jackson, Anne, 171
Jackson, Barry, 80
Jagger, Dean, 102
Jeans, Ursula, 36
Johnson, Celia, 121
Johnson, Van, 161
Jones, Jennifer, 122, 154, 155
Joseph And His Brethren, 177
The Journey, 170-2, 173

Kane, Robert, 47-8
Kaufman, George, 77, 163
Keller, Helen, 124
Kennedy, John F., 177
Kennedy, Robert, 176-7
Kerr, Deborah, 117, 121, 125, 171, 172
King, Dennis, 125
King, Nelson, 28
King, Mrs Nelson (Nora), 28-9, 31-2, 33
Kingston, Jeremy, 189
Korda, Alexander, 152, 156
Kossoff, David, 171

Lambert, J.W., 146
Landis, Carole, 118-19
Langley, Noel, 63, 108, 115
The Last of Mrs Cheyney, 26
The Late George Apsley, 123
Late Night Final, 33
Laughton, Charles, 51, 62, 74, 89, 151
Lawrence, Gertrude, 120, 129, 147
Lean, David, 64
Lefaux, Charles, 48
Lejeune, C.A., 69, 156
Lemmy, Dr, master of Wellesley House, 17
Letts, Pauline, 43, 50, 68, 109, 110-11, 117

Levin, Bernard, 173, 174
Lewin, David, 146
Libel, 173
A Likely Tale, 164-5
Lillie, Beatrice, 100-1, 124
Limpus, Alban, 34
Lingstrom, Miss, 150
Little, Charles, 191
Little, Daisy, 193
The Little Hut, 142, 144-7, 149, 150,
  151, 153, 154
Litvak, Anatole, 172, 173
Lollobrigida, Gina, 154
Lombard, Carole, 57
Lonsdale, Freddie, 124
Lorre, Peter, 154
The Love Doctor, 174
The Loved One, 181

McCulloch, Ian, 188
MacDonald, Jeanette, 57
McGrath, Leueen, 111, 163
Major Barbara, 81-2, 84, 86-7, 91-2
A Majority of One, 174, 175
The Man Who Came To Dinner, 77, 94-6,
  97, 98-100, 175
Maney, Richard, 121
Mann, Roderick, 146
Many Waters, 29
Marcus, Frank, 186
Margaret, Princess, 160, 161
*Maria Marten or The Murder in the
  Red Barn*, 43
Marie Antoinette, 54-6, 58, 60-2, 64,
  65, 67, 69
Marion-Crawford, Howard, 156
Marshall, Norman, 30, 44-5, 46, 65,
  103, 110
Mary, Queen, 117
Massey, Raymond, 66, 70
Matthews, A.E., 36, 74
Mayer, Louis B., 54, 60-1, 62, 75, 127
Menzies, Robert, 135
Mercouri, Melina, 181
Merivale, Philip, 80
Merivale, Ros, 82
Merrall, Mary, 68, 80
Messel, Oliver, 145
Midgely, Robin, 188
Miller, Gilbert, 64, 66, 67, 76, 79, 81,

110, 119, 121, 122, 124, 125, 129,
  130
Mills, John, 97
Minster, Barbara (*née* Cochran), 79,
  80
Minister, Jack, 78, 79, 89, 90, 100
Misalliance, 175
Mitford, Nancy, 144, 145
Moore, Eva, 23
Morley, Alexis, 185, 193
Morley, Annabel, 108, 118, 127, 128
  130, 135, 147, 150, 151, 152, 155,
  176, 188, 191, 193
Morley, Gertrude Emily (*née* Fass;
  'Daisy'), 10-11, 12, 13, 14, 15, 19,
  21, 26, 31, 33, 37, 52, 63, 64, 65, 69,
  83, 84, 118, 160, 162
Morley, Hugo, 182, 193
Morley, Joan (*née* Buckmaster), 78,
  79-86, 87, 89, 90, 92-3, 95-6, 99,
  101, 108, 110, 113, 116, 118, 120-1,
  122-3, 125, 126, 127-8, 130, 134,
  138-9, 141-2, 146, 147, 152, 155,
  157, 168, 171, 188
Morley, Margaret ('Cissie'), 9,
  11-12, 13, 14, 15, 21, 83, 118
Morley, Major Robert Wilton, 10-11,
  12, 13-15, 19, 21, 91
Morley, Sheridan, 95-6, 104, 118,
  127, 133, 135, 140, 141, 147-8,
  150, 153, 155, 170, 176, 183
Morley, Wilton, 150-1, 153, 155, 176,
  185, 188, 193, 194
Mosely, Leonard, 161
Mr Rhodes, 178
Mundy, Meg, 122
Murray, Barbara, 170

Nares, Owen, 72
Nash, Roy, 151
Neagle, Anna, 102, 116
Neville, John, 173
Nine Hours To Rama, 178
Niven, David, 156
Norgate, Matthew, 46
Novello, Ivor, 72, 124

The Old Dark House, 180
Oliver Twist, 175
Olivier, Laurence, 46, 53, 66, 156,
  187

Once More With Feeling, 173
One Pair of Eyes, 184
Orchard, Julian, 167, 168-9, 191-2
Oscar Wilde, 44-6, 50, 63, 64-7, 69, 72,
  73, 74-5, 76, 77, 79, 110, 121, 124,
  148, 176, 192
Outcast of the Islands, 148, 151, 176
Owen, Frank, 94

Page, Norman, 25
Pagnol, Marcel, 166
Palmer, Lilli, 118
Parent-Craft, 149-50
Pascal, Gabriel, 81-2, 84, 86-7, 91
Paul, Jeremy, 184
Percy, Edward, 89, 90
Percy, Esme, 15
Perranporth Players, Cornwall
  (summer theatre), 41-3, 49-50, 51,
  60, 62-3, 67, 76-8
Perrick, Eve, 161
Petingell, Frank, 45
Phillpotts, Ambrosine, 80-1, 84, 89,
  90-1, 98-9, 100-1, 111, 143, 154,
  182, 189-90
Phipps, Nick, 79, 80
Pickford, Mary, 108
Picon, Molly, 174, 175
A Picture of Innocence, 194
Play With Fire, 89-91, 92-3, 95, 98
Plowright, Joan, 172
Porter, Cole, 120
Powell, Dilys, 91
Power, Tyrone, 62
Proust, Colette, 158
Pygmalion, 51, 75

Raglan, Robert, 184
The Rainbow Jacket, 160
The Rape of the Belt, 170
Ratoff, Gregory, 176
Rattigan, Terence, 153, 156
Redgrave, Michael, 161
Redman, Joyce, 150
Reed, Carol, 97, 118, 141, 148
Reed, Tracy, 177
Rees, Llewellyn ('Lulu'), 53-4, 55,
  56, 57, 58-9, 60, 61, 68, 70-1, 76,
  77, 78, 79, 82, 83, 88, 116-17
Richard, Cliff, 178

Richards, Dick, 173
Richardson, Sir Ralph, 148, 176
Richardson, Tony, 181
The Road To Hong Kong, 178
Robert Morley: Responsible Gentleman,
  182
Robin Fox Partnership, 169-70,
  173-4, 178
Rome, Harold, 166
Roosevelt, Eleanor, 176
Rostand, Maurice, 44
Roussin, André, 144, 157, 172
Royal Academy of Dramatic Art,
  21, 22-6, 138, 160
Russell, Fred, 120
Rutherford, Margaret, 36, 152, 164,
  165

Salome, 30
Sanders, George, 125
Saroyan, William, 120
Savoury, Gerald, 164
Seastrom (Sjostrom), Victor, 47, 50
Selznick, David, 155
Seyler, Athene, 144
Shakespeare, William, 30-1
Shaw, George Bernard, 15, 25, 27,
  51, 75, 84, 87, 104, 175
Shearer, Norma, 51, 53, 54, 55, 58,
  60, 62, 69, 75
Shephard, Firth, 94
Sherek, Henry, 73, 88, 89, 99, 104,
  105-7, 108, 109, 110, 111, 113,
  114-15, 116, 119-20, 121, 124, 125,
  157
Sherek, Pamela, 104
Sherwood, Robert, 70
Short Story, 34-9, 86, 91
Shulman, Milton, 151, 173
Sinclair, Hugh, 68
Sisson, Rosemary Anne, 188-9
Six Months' Grace, 169-70
The Sound of Morley, 182
Springtime for Henry, 43
Staff Dance, 34, 98, 100-1, 124
Stars at Midnight (Palladium gala),
  156
Stewart, Athole, 23
Stewart, Donald, Ogden, 117
Stewart, Jimmy, 62

205

Stewart, Sophie, 132
Stokes, Leslie, 44-5
Stokes, Sewell, 44-6, 49, 63, 65, 71, 72, 74, 75, 76, 77, 82, 84, 96, 126, 143, 181, 193
The Story of Gilbert and Sullivan, 152, 156
Stromberg, Hunt, 51
Stubbs, Nancy (nanny), 118, 123, 125, 134, 141, 142, 150
Sunday Night at the Palladium, 170

Tait, John, 125, 138
Tempest, Marie, 34-5, 36-7, 38, 39, 54, 85-6
Temple, Shirley, 57
Tendre Voyou, 181
Tetzel, Joan, 145, 150, 186
Thalberg, Irving, 54
This Was Paris, 94
Thorndike, Russel, 28
Thorndyke, Sybil, 36-7, 39, 160
Thurber, James, 173
Tierney, Gene, 71
A Time To Laugh, 178-9
To See Ourselves, 42-3
Todd, Ann, 162-3
Tomlinson, David, 145, 153
Tone, Franchot, 60
Too Many Chefs, 193
Topkapi, 180-1
Tracy, Spencer, 75, 116, 117, 121-2, 125
Treasure Island, 24-5
Truman, Harry, S., 122
The Tunnel of Love, 170
Tutin, Dorothy, 173
Tuyn, Harry, 148
Tynan, Kenneth, 165

Under The Red Robe, 47, 50
Upton, Ted, 111
Ustinov, Peter, 162, 180, 182

Van Dyke, W.S. ('Woody'), 55-6, 58
Vanbrugh, Irene, 25
Vanbrugh, Violet, 24
Vanderbilt, Mrs, 74
Viertel, Peter, 172

Wallace, Ian, 166, 167
Ward, Tony, 138
Wardle, Irving, 142
Waterman, John, 173
Watts, Richard, Jr., 67
Waugh, Evelyn, 102
Welles, Orson, 117
Wellington College, 16-19
Wells, John, 194
What's My Line?, 157-8
When Eight Bells Toll, 184
Wilcox, Herbert, 101-2, 116
Wilding, Michael, 116
Williams, Emlyn, 98, 181
Williamson, J.C., Organization, 125, 130, 131, 133, 134
Wilson, Cecil, 169
Wimperis, Arthur, 119
Winnington, Richard, 151
Wolfit, Donald, 161
Woolcott, Alexander, 77, 94-5, 96
Worth, Irene, 111, 118
Wraight, Robert, 165, 174
Wynyard, Diana, 51

You Will Remember, 92
The Young Mr Pitt, 97-8
The Young Ones, 178